# EXPANDING Literacy

Brett Pierce

# EXPANDING Literacy

## Bringing Digital Storytelling into Your Classroom

Heinemann
Portsmouth, NH

**Heinemann**
145 Maplewood Avenue, Suite 300
Portsmouth, NH 03801
www.heinemann.com



The author and publisher wish to thank those who have generously given permission to reprint borrowed material:

"5 Reasons to Integrate Digital Storytelling into Your Teaching" by Matt Loera and Heather Sinclair from *eSchool News* website, uploaded August 29, 2019, https://www.eschoolnews.com/2019/08/29/5-reasons-to-integrate-digital-storytelling-into-your-teaching/2/.

Excerpts from Common Core State Standards © Copyright 2010. National Governors Association Center for Best Practices and Council of Chief State School Officers. All rights reserved.

**Images**
Figure 4.4: Photographs by Kerry Michaels.

**Library of Congress Cataloging-in-Publication Data**
Names: Pierce, Brett, author.
Title: Expanding literacy : bringing digital storytelling into your classroom / Brett Pierce.
Description: Portsmouth, NH : Heinemann Publishing, 2022. | Includes bibliographical references.
Identifiers: LCCN 2021051281 | ISBN 9780325132396
Subjects: LCSH: Composition (Language arts)—Study and teaching (Secondary) | Digital storytelling.
Classification: LCC LB1631.3. P54 2022 | DDC 372.67/7044—dc23/eng/20211213
LC record available at https://lccn.loc.gov/2021051281

**Editor:** Louisa Irele
**Production Editors:** Sean Moreau and Patty Adams
**Cover and Interior Designer:** Vita Lane
**Typesetter:** Gina Poirier Design
**Manufacturing:** Val Cooper

Printed in the United States of America on acid-free paper
1 2 3 4 5 CGB 26 25 24 23 22 PO# 34005

To Kerry, whose love propelled me into and sustained me during this endeavor. And to our kids—Ethan and Maya—who gave me years of excuses to indulge in stories and storytelling. All three of you form the ebullient universe that allows me to think, express, and reach. And dance . . . Bouncing Around the Room.

And to my mom and dad, who gave me full latitude to follow my passions and instincts, with nary a cocked head or raised eyebrow.

# Contents

# Digital Storytelling Activities

# Acknowledgments

I want to begin by thanking a few Meridian Stories board members who have guided me from the start of this journey into classroom digital storytelling, and they include Fiona Wilson, Christina Finneran, Sarah Childress, an1d Kathy Biberstein. Additionally, a few who have been supportive at pivotal moments include Charlotte Cole, a tried-and-true colleague of many years who joined forces with me to research the efficacy of the approach championed in this book, and Bob Moore, who helped me bring digital storytelling to life in schools toward the start of this endeavor. Educators who have enthusiastically embraced Meridian Stories over the years include Beth Alden, Ell Fanus, Emily Higgins, Heather Sinclair, Darren Joyce, Ginny Brackett, and Barbara Slote. Thanks as well to Louisa Irele, my Heinemann editor, who has graciously, respectfully, and insightfully crafted a pathway forward with this content. And finally, I'd like to reacknowledge the support of my family, to whom this book is dedicated: Kerry, Ethan, and Maya.

# EXPANDING Literacy

CHAPTER ONE

# The Rationale for Making Digital Storytelling a Normative Classroom Practice

The world of digital storytelling revealed itself to me in a simple incident involving my son when he was in seventh grade. He had stayed the weekend at a friend's house and they had spent the entire time making a video to post to their new Facebook accounts. This was around 2011. They posted the video, and for the first time, my son was getting likes and encouraging comments from his classmates. This meant the world to him.

Then I heard murmuring among parents in the bleachers at a middle school basketball game. Had I seen the video? Ummm, no. I went home and watched it. It was making fun of Justin Bieber and was . . . offensive. It had some clever comic edits; I was impressed, honestly, but appalled at the same time. Here I was, a producer and program developer for Sesame Workshop, the creators of *Sesame Street*. My job was to help people make short videos about curricular goals in order to educate children and youth. My job was to invest in the idea that the stories we tell in the media—the characters we create—can positively affect attitudes and behavior in our audiences. But in my own backyard, my sensitive and conscientious son had made a funny video that was increasing his popularity while reinforcing derogatory stereotypes—a trade-off that was a no-brainer to a thirteen-year-old. This moment brought to the light of day what had been slowly churning under the surface: professional media makers like myself who go through painstakingly detailed processes to produce media that will positively affect human thinking and behavior were being replaced by a new tsunami of programming that was being created and disseminated by . . . anyone with a smartphone. The universal democratization of media creation had an emerging dark side. Was there anything I could do to address it?

The answer was yes: find a way to make meaningful, thoughtful digital storytelling a standard, best practice in schools. That's what writing a school paper is all about—organizing ideas to tell a coherent and meaningful story. So, why not transfer that complex set of skills to digital storytelling so those same standards could be applied to the emergent digital world of stories that was consuming youth's daily hours?

A simple proposition to self, and I got excited. I had spent over twenty years at Sesame Workshop as a producer in the international department. This meant that I got to work with existing TV formats—*Square One TV* (a math show), *3–2–1 Contact* (a science show), and *Ghostwriter* (a literacy show)—and adapt them to the local culture in full collaboration with local producers. These shows all saw new and distinctly different lives in countries like Indonesia, Israel, China, the United Kingdom, and Poland. And this work expanded as time went on. I was an executive producer on a series about "intercultural understanding, conflict prevention in a multicultural setting, and conflict resolution in children's everyday lives and circumstances" that targeted youth ages eight through twelve in what is now North Macedonia. I was a cocreator and producer of *Salam Shabab*, a series targeting Iraqi youth ages thirteen through eighteen that ran for three seasons and was designed to "create the foundations of peace building by empowering Iraqi youth to be confident, open-minded and participatory citizens of a diverse society."

This proposition to self asked me to take this process of curriculum-driven media creation and bring it into the classroom, which is where I began my career: teaching high school English in Virginia.

As the first concrete step in this educational odyssey, I started Meridian Stories (www.meridianstories.com), a nonprofit with a mission "to prepare middle and high school students for the 21st century workplace by providing opportunities to collaborate, create, problem solve, and lead in the development and production of meaningful digital narratives that address curricular goals" (Pierce 2010).

That was ten years ago. The experience of this book is fed by the connections I've made to middle and high school teachers and students through Meridian Stories over the past ten years; by the continued international work I do in places like the United Arab Emirates, Somalia, and South Sudan, where we work together to create digital stories—audio and video—for social impact; and by my annual teaching in the Jan Plan at Colby College, where I have the privilege to teach a course called Developing Media for Social Change.

I am a classroom teacher but mostly an outsider to the daily dictates of life in middle and high school. However, I am a full-on educator (BA in theatre, MA in literature, EdM in communications) who hopes that in bringing this media-based perspective into the classroom, we can allow creative sparks to fly and begin to formulate a paradigm shift to the full integration of meaningful digital storytelling into the classroom.

# The Setting: A Glancing Peek into Our Digitized World

Only a few times in the history of humankind have societies shifted entirely as a result of the introduction of a new medium or communication technology. We are amid one of those times, and this book is about teaching to the new form of writing that is emerging as a result.

But let's start with some context. Way, way, way back when, we shifted from oral cultures to literate cultures. The origins of writing can be traced to the late fourth millennium BC, when, some scholars argue, it began as a result of an increasingly complex economy in Mesopotamia, where transactions could no longer be memorized: they had to be recorded in some fashion (Robinson 2007). The nature of this change is eloquently articulated by Walter Ong, a breakthrough scholar in this realm who had this to say about orality:

> **In an oral culture, knowledge, once acquired, had to be constantly repeated or it would be lost: fixed, formulaic thought patterns were essential for wisdom and effective administration. . . . Without writing, words . . . have no visual presence, even when the objects they represent are visual. . . . They have no focus and no trace, not even a trajectory. They are occurrences, events. (1982, 23–31)**

Words as actions. Not descriptions of actions, but actions themselves. I love that idea. Then came print, and here is what Walter Ong has to say about that:

> **Writing separates the knower from the known and thus sets up conditions for "objectivity" in the sense of personal disengagement or distancing. . . . To live and understand fully, we need not only proximity but also distance. This writing provides for consciousness as nothing else does. (1982, 45–82)**

Heavy stuff. But so cool. And this just scratches at the surface of how writing changed humanity's relationship to self and society. Jump ahead over five thousand years to 1450 AD and we got the printing press—the next significant innovation in the interdependence between humanity and media. With the printing press, among other things, knowledge was democratized as literacy became widespread; the nation state was born now that laws and rules could be printed, disseminated, and enforced; and language was standardized.

Fast-forward to the start of the twentieth century, and radio, followed by TV, entered into society's mainstream, reshaping how we spent time and interacted, expanding our understanding of the larger world, and introducing the idea of culturally shared experiences: everyone growing up in the sixties and seventies knew Walter Cronkite, *Bewitched*, and *The Jeffersons*. The introduction of television and radio dramatically reconfigured the way we thought, perceived, interacted, and understood, and all of this was foreseen in the midsixties by Marshall McLuhan, who famously wrote: "For the 'message' of any medium or technology is the change of scale or pace or pattern that it introduces into human affairs" (1964, 1).

Look at that statement. For me, those words contain an idea that is infinite in its range and therefore scary, profound, exciting, and enlightening. My translation: communication technologies universally reprogram our understanding of self and others and communities and societies, and the more aware we are of this phenomenon, the better able we are to harness and optimize those changes.

And now we have the internet, which has in turn yielded the many social media platforms of which we are all well aware.

I mention all this not as groundbreaking news, but as a reminder that (1) history has proven that the introduction of communication technologies does indeed change how societies evolve, and (2) we are currently living through one of those seismic societal conversions that used to take hundreds of years—the impact of the printing press, for example—and is now reduced to a matter of a few years.

One telling lens through which to gain a perspective on this phenomenon is through the four reports that Common Sense Media has produced between 2011 and 2020 on media use and access among zero- to eight-year-olds. The excerpts in Figure 1–1 illustrate the speed and depth with which digital culture is seeping into our lives. There are monumental changes in behavior happening every couple of years. I have chosen these reports that highlight this age group because the kids from this study are your current or near-future students. But the larger point is this: just look at the movement of media use in terms of availability and consumption over the ten-year period shown in Figure 1-1.

---

**Figure 1–1**

## 2011

Today a substantial proportion of the time that young children spend with screen media is spent with digital media—including computers, handheld and console video game players, and other interactive mobile devices such as cell phones, video iPods, and iPad-style tablet devices. Among 0- to 8-year-olds as a whole, a quarter (27%) of all screen time is spent with these digital devices. (Rideout 2011, 9)

### 2013

Among families with children age 8 and under, there has been a five-fold increase in ownership of tablet devices such as iPads, from 8% of all families in 2011 to 40% in 2013. (Rideout 2013, 9)

### 2017

Nearly all (98 percent) children age 8 and under live in a home with some type of mobile device. . . . The average amount of time spent with mobile devices each day has tripled (again). (Rideout 2017, 3)

### 2020

For the first time, watching online videos on sites like YouTube now constitutes the largest proportion of children's total TV and video viewing. (Rideout and Robb 2020, 4)

---

Just how pervasive is YouTube in the lives of youth, and why does it matter to educators? According to a 2018 Pew Research Center study, 85 percent of teens say they use YouTube the most of any social media platform out there (Anderson and Jiang 2018). A 2019 Common Sense Media Report confirms this: "YouTube clearly dominates the online video space among both tweens and teens" (Rideout and Mann 2019, 4). This makes sense considering that, according to YouTube itself, in 2020, it had more than two billion logged-in users per month and "more than 500 hours of content . . . uploaded . . . every minute" (YouTube n.d.).

Every minute. Simply mind-blowing. What do we suppose is one of the compelling factors driving this massive appeal among youth?

Character. On YouTube, they are called YouTubers or influencers.

Research is currently being conducted about why kids see relationships with YouTubers as more significant than relationships with the people around them. This is a real thing. Reflect on that for a beat: a phenomenon is emerging whereby kids trust and embrace their chosen influencer over the family and friends in their physical community. One reason, reports Dr. Grant Brenner in a blog post for *Psychology Today*, is this: "Arguably, for many people, asymmetrical relationships with YouTubers can be a huge saving grace, therapeutic, and potentially an emotionally and physically safer alternative than actual human beings" (2019). Here are these youth (the influencers), looking directly at you (the viewer); speaking to you in the intimacy of wherever you watch your computer or phone; helping you in how to be cool and confident and socially knowledgeable, but doing so in a way that is unscripted—that is, "real"—and that hints at vulnerability. In short, it's what you want from a good friend: honesty, trust, and confidentiality. And all at no personal or social cost to you. It's a huge win-win.

Let's go one step further down this road. LEGO, in 2019, in an effort to "inspire the next generation of space exploration," conducted a survey of over three thousand kids, ages eight through twelve, about their interest in becoming astronauts. You know what the surveyors found out instead? They discovered that "today's children are three times more likely to aspire to be a YouTuber (29%) than an Astronaut (11%)" (LEGO Group 2019). YouTubers have the status of celebrities, but here's the catch: it's a brand of celebrity that is within reach of everyone with a digital camera in their phone or computer. This isn't traditional celebrity worshipping to excite and enthrall. This is celebrity intimacy to model and to which to aspire.

These select nuggets are just a few existential stars in the formative galaxy that is YouTube . . . and TikTok . . . and . . . to be determined. It is clearly a massive phenomenon in the lives of our students, but the question remains: Why does it matter to educators?

Here is the answer: YouTube is the vast Alexandrian Library for our time. For baby boomers or Gen Xers, the libraries tend to be traditional. The Library of Congress, Oxford's Bodleian Library, the New York Public Library in New York City—these are among humanity's great repositories of information and knowledge. However, for millennials and for your students, the great repository of information and knowledge lives on phones. It's where they go for information, how-tos, comedy, music, entertainment, and, it appears, socializing. Now, think of your local library. What do you go there for? The answer: information, how-tos, comedy, music, entertainment, and, sometimes, socializing. Same purposes. Different destinations.

## The Action: What Is Digital Storytelling?

Digital storytelling is the capacity to communicate using text, sound, music, and imagery—still and moving. You don't have to use all of these tools, but they are the main components of digital storytelling. If we think of this in terms of primary and secondary colors, then text, sound, music, and imagery are your primary colors. Pacing, visual palette, graphics, voice, tone, and genre (comedy, game show, news, mystery, etc.) might be your secondary colors. It's a relatively vast range of tools with which to work in order to effectively communicate. And in that range lies both its complexity and wonder, its challenge and opportunity.

Historically in the United States and throughout Western cultures, the primary source of information has been print-based. That is most of humanity's traditional literacy. That is the basis of our entire education system. But print-based literacy, for middle and high school students, is generally exciting only for those that have a solid command of language and ideas. And according to the National Assessment of Educational Progress (NAEP), that number is only about 37 percent of twelfth graders and 34 percent of eighth graders. Those are the percentages that the NAEP deems are "at or above proficient" in reading (2019). This means that over 60 percent of our students are at basic or below-basic reading. The figures are roughly equivalent for "writing," although the latest figures from NAEP, as of the writing of this book, are from 2011.

I fully support the argument that textual literacy is an important skill set that allows us to organize our thoughts, build arguments, communicate concisely, research, and validate theses.

However, I also believe that textual literacy—the organizing of ideas through words and sentence structure; the command of language—is of equal educational value to digital literacy. The two literacies don't compete but instead complement and energize each other.

So, what exactly is *digital literacy*? In what will be a repeating format throughout this book, I asked this question to a range of middle and high school teachers from the United States. Here are some of their answers.

Clearly, there is no simple, definitive understanding of this phrase. For me, Emily comes closest. It's both the capacity to understand information and knowledge that is represented digitally—what is often the primary focus of the phrase "media literacy"—*and* the capacity to create information

## What is Digital Literacy?

**Alyssa:** Yeah, that one I hadn't really heard before; I don't know. . . . So you're tech-friendly, basically.

**Tamiko:** To me, digital literacy would be the ability to discern and use technology to get information and your perspective clearly defined to another person.

**Andrea:** For me, it's they're on a computer whether it's alone or in a small group where they're using some form of media to help them read or to help them comprehend . . . or something like that.

**Bill:** I would presume that digital literacy is, like, your ability to successfully use modern-day technology like the internet and smartphones and different platforms? Am I close?

**Darren:** Digital literacy . . . means to me the ability to communicate through the medium of audio and visual technology.

**Todd:** The first thing that comes to my mind is guiding students in how to exactly produce content across digital means.

**Emily:** I think digital literacy is the . . . it's almost like, um, I have a couple of different definitions in my mind. One definition would be understanding information that's out there and determining how it can be used and the veracity of that. But there's also the digital literacy piece of being able to use technology in a way that you choose. Part of digital literacy is being able to push a button and not be petrified with what is going to happen.

**Ell:** It is the ability to use digital tools to communicate in a language that integrates many languages. An international language. That's the gist.

and knowledge utilizing a range of digital tools. In other words, it's a new form of reading and writing.

Despite the lack of clarity about this phrase among teachers, the National Council of Teachers of English (NCTE), in November 2019, took the dramatic step of redefining what is meant by *literacy* in a position statement carrying the headline "Definition of Literacy in a Digital Age." While the definition is long with many bullet points, it begins with this introductory note:

> **Literacy has always been a collection of communicative and sociocultural practices shared among communities. As society and technology change, so does literacy. The world demands that a literate person possess and intentionally apply a wide range of skills, competencies, and dispositions. These literacies are interconnected, dynamic, and malleable. As in the past, they are inextricably linked with histories, narratives, life possibilities, and social trajectories of all individuals and groups.**

This opening statement does so much. It acknowledges technology as one of two drivers of change in our understanding of this term. It acknowledges a new and "malleable" form of literacy. It acknowledges multiple literacies. It acknowledges a literacy that "the world demands." Think about that. The world has always aimed for a high degree of literacy, as we understand that term traditionally. But now, according to the NCTE, the world "demands" it.

I fully agree.

The writing part of this literacy is digital storytelling, the subject of this book. And this new writing opens up tremendous opportunities for vastly more than the 37 percent who are "proficient" or "advanced" text writers. Why? Because digital storytelling is visual. Digital storytelling is aural. And digital storytelling is dynamic: it moves . . . literally. In digital storytelling, swaths of new pathways to communicate effectively and meaningfully become available. And for educators, this is unbelievably exciting.

The question that propels this book forward is this: Are we preparing our kids to be meaningful contributors to this digitally literate universe? If the dialogue that propels our current culture is primarily happening inside of a digital platform that subsists on a mix of text, sound, music, and imagery, then our students need to be prepared to be productive and articulate participants on this digital platform. They need to be substantive digital creators—storytellers.

# Digital Storytelling and Educational Equity

The complex issue of educational equity, which largely revolves around the concepts of fairness, inclusion, and access, is a vital and necessary framework within which to assess any new educational proposition. I believe that digital storytelling is one indispensable asset in the educational equity tool kit. The primary reason is that digital storytelling provides multiple pathways into (1) effective communication; (2) learning engagement; and (3) voice amplification.

In the first area, the simple truth is that digital storytelling does not rely on a command of the English language in order to communicate in a meaningful and substantive manner. We know that language proficiency can be an overwhelming barrier to educational equity. This is especially true for all those in the United States for whom English is not their native language. But it's also true for those for whom writing—with the complexity of its component parts, from grammar to spelling, vocabulary to hypothesis creation—is a pervasive struggle and will never be the preferred mode of communication. The "language" of digital storytelling is, on the other hand, universal: it's imagery, music, sound, and yes, words, but not words that have to exist in a formally correct sentence to be fully understood.

Second, digital storytelling is a process that naturally invites a wide range of expertise and interests. A good digital story may require a good logistics person (the producer), a storyteller (the writer), an imaginative mind (the story creator or writer), a technology person (the camera person, the editor, the sound person), an investigator to find all those royalty-free images (the researcher), a dramatic person (the actor), and a computer programmer (graphics creator and editor). In short, at the core of digital storytelling creation is a diverse set of skills that may reflect the diverse interests in your classroom. There's an inviting portal for just about everyone—a window into the possibility of academic engagement and success for all.

Third, digital storytelling is, by its very nature, a social activity. It is organically designed to be shared with a wider audience—an audience outside of the classroom. The distribution platforms and the content—the story—are component parts of a whole communication experience. This is a critical point to understand. In the practice of digital storytelling, the experience of literacy is no longer an isolated one between the student and the teacher. It's public. It's social. The very first bullet point in the NCTE's wide-ranging definition of "literacy in a digital age" is "participate effectively and critically in a networked world" (2019). It's about the participation. And where there is participation in a larger "networked world," there is an exponentially increased chance to be heard, to have a voice: to even the playing field.

Let's unpack that idea for a beat.

# Digital Storytelling and a Participatory Culture: Amplifying Student Voice

The ability to be seen or heard used to come from the top down—*from* the publishers and broadcasters *to* the people. Now it comes from the bottom up. Let's go back to YouTube. YouTube is operating in our time in the same revolutionary capacity as the printing press between 1500 and 1800: it is vastly expanding ordinary people's access to literacy. Except that in terms of impact, while the printing press democratized reading, YouTube is democratizing publishing. That's right. Everyone can be viewed and heard—published or broadcast, as it were—free of charge. The relevance of digital literacy—digital storytelling, in particular—isn't simply an organic consequence of the rise of technology. No. It's a response to the creation of digital platforms where the majority of youth are residing—to be with their friends, to laugh, to find new heroes, to learn . . . and to be heard.

This new nonhierarchical media culture was anticipated back in 2005 with the publication of *Deep Focus: A Report on the Future of Independent Media* (Blau).

> The media landscape will be reshaped by the bottom-up energy of media created by amateurs and hobbyists as a matter of course. . . . Images, ideas, news, and points of view will come from everywhere and travel along countless new routes to an ever-growing number of places where they can be viewed. This bottom-up energy will radiate enormous energy and creativity, but it will also tear apart some of the categories that organize the lives and work of media makers. . . . A new generation of media makers and viewers is emerging, which could lead to a sea change in how media is made and received.

Henry Jenkins, one of America's foremost media scholars, introduced the phrase "participatory culture" back in 2006 when he glimpsed the possibilities that media creation would be flipped on its head. He wrote, "The new media literacies should be seen as social skills, as ways of interacting within a larger community, and not simply an individualized skill to be used for personal expression."

There it is, right there: digital literacy as a "social skill" and a new way of "interacting with a larger community." Digital storytelling is indeed the primary and continually emerging way for youth to both socialize and interact with their community. The gatekeepers of storytelling have been deposed. Goodbye, CBS, NBC, ABC, and Fox as the sole shapers of news. Goodbye, Penguin Random House, Hachette, and HarperCollins as the exclusive curators of what should be read. It's a bottom-up world of publishing, and the main form of that publishing is . . . digital stories. Instagram stories are digital stories. Facebook posts: digital stories. Podcasts: digital stories. YouTube: five hundred hours of content uploaded every minute. All digital stories. Every minute!

And emerging from the leviathan that is YouTube is . . . TikTok. TikTok takes YouTube and utterly socializes it. Personalizes it. Expands it, but within a small sphere of storytelling. Whether it's the go-to place at the time you are reading this book or not doesn't matter. It's an example of a digital storytelling variant (word of the year in 2021) that has washed over youth and shifted their screen time to a new platform with its simple focus on this idea that "authenticity is king" (TikTok 2020).

Has there ever been a more all-consuming and far-reaching literacy? Has the need to teach toward writing fluency in this literacy ever been greater?

Students, for the first time in history, have a variety of media platforms to amplify their voices. It's our job as educators to teach our students to tell meaningful and impactful stories that can become significant contributions to this infinitely expanding digital universe of content. This is especially imperative in our age of misinformation and disinformation. I would argue that teaching youth how to tell meaningful stories can be a pivotal strategy against the pervasiveness of misinformation. That is a line of inquiry that won't be developed in these pages, but I believe it's an important facet of digital storytelling to consider.

In the end, the digital realm is their library. It's their communication platform. It's their social life. It's their source of knowledge. It's their language. It's a full-blown communication spectrum, the breadth and depth of which is unprecedented in history. And this communication spectrum requires literacy: the ability to read it and write for it. I repeat the question that propels this book forward: Are we preparing our kids to be meaningful contributors in this digitally literate universe? Are we teaching them to write effectively inside of this literacy?

I don't think we are. Is it even possible, given the infinitely changing nature of digital communication?

## The Conflict: Can We Teach This Without Formal Training?

Digital storytelling may involve skill sets that you, the educator, may not have. There are video production and sound editing as well as rules about use of existing imagery and creative common licenses, in which you may hardly be an expert. There are apps that you may not know about or use, and there are uploads and downloads that, well, never seem to work without bringing in the IT specialist. In short, for some teachers, digital storytelling puts them at a huge disadvantage, forcing them to yield classroom control and exposing their perceived technological weaknesses.

There actually is a simple answer to this: *you don't need to know any of that stuff.* All you need to know is what you know: the content. The answer to any question from the students about digital production and IT-related questions is this: "You figure it out." Here's the reality. In traditional text-based literacy, you, the educator, know the rules and you teach those rules to your students, whether you are teaching science, math, history, or literature. Text-based literacy is powered by rules of syntax and grammar, word choice and punctuation. Digital literacy is not about rules as much as it about mechanics. Digital literacy is about knowing (1) the individual operations of the different digital parts (imagery, music, sound, editing, zooms, etc.) and (2) how those different digital parts all synchronize with each other. For the students, allowing them to discover these digital mechanics—including cool apps that let letters fly or distort an image to comic effect—is like letting them loose in a playground designed just for them. Except it's digital.

Like TikTok. One of the reasons TikTok is so appealing is that all of these digital mechanics are packaged in one place and can be manipulated with a touch or a swipe. TikTok has a Creator Portal that includes special effects, a library of sounds and transitions, editing tips, and suggestions for where to spot the latest visual trends. It's all prepackaged. Everything you need. It's designed like a personalized digital playground and operates as one. If you do have students that feel fully stymied by the production piece of digital storytelling, suggest that they start on TikTok: it's the bunny slope of digital production.

Discovering the various components of digital literacy is part of the learning experience. Teaching you, the educator, what they, the students, have discovered, is also a vital part of the learning experience. We all know the power of this flipped classroom model, even in this micro format. But it still takes guts and confidence to yield that control of information and knowledge.

However, the payoff is huge.

# The Cliff-Hanger: A Culture of Omnipresent Change

Before we dive into the educational luxuries afforded by digital storytelling, we have to ask one more essential question. The nature of the postsecondary professional world is changing rapidly. Education is fundamentally based on preparing students for a somewhat predictable working environment. That predictability is evaporating. So, given the dramatic changes society is undergoing, for what are we preparing our students?

The answer: a culture of omnipresent change.

OK, cool. Ummm, but how the hell do we do that?! What does this even mean? How do you prepare students for a world that one can't envision because it's constantly shifting? This vast unknown has sixth-grade teacher Andrea Scharmer on edge: "The thought of where everything is now versus when I started teaching is very different. And the things that kids are exposed to now are so different. I mean, I can't even imagine ten years from now what that's even going to look like."

## Teachers and the Need for Technological or Media Command

**Morgan:** I will tell you this: if anyone tells you that they don't know how to use the media, that is not true at all. Kids are better than I am at the end of their time after using it and I think that is a powerful piece for them.

**Todd:** I often say that: just play around with it. That's part of learning the technology is troubleshooting. I tell them, "I've learned so much because I have run into so many problems. So, what can you do to try and find a way around this problem?" Some kids are willing to persevere through that, but other kids, like a lot of learning situations, cave into the frustrations, quickly. . . . You are going to encounter obstacles or fail miserably, but what are you taking away from that or what did you learn from that experience?

**Heather:** I would say that my knowledge of media production and digital storytelling skills is growing but is not spectacularly deep. I don't have any formal training in production, in a digital or electronic format. . . . Knowing how to ask the good question and then encouraging my students to find the resources, and then a lot of it becomes trial and error, and it's just become a part of the process. So, it hasn't slowed me down. It's just become a way of encouraging my students to become masters of whatever skill it is that they're looking for.

**Darren:** Students managed themselves just fine, especially when they knew I would be of little help. I played dumb with technology but did give little hints along the way. The school-provided technology was not helpful for this project; almost all the work was done on students' phones, which they loved using as a tool. . . . I think they have been saturated with this since they were born, from PBS Kids all the way up to TikTok now. I figured that they were the better experts on this than I would be.

**Emily:** The technology piece is not an obstacle to me or any other teachers when doing digital storytelling projects. Teachers think it is but my students have always been better at it than me. And even when they haven't been that good at it, they are more than happy to help each other figure out how to do stuff. Because there is always someone in your class that has done stop-motion animation or likes to splice together things, often not in the best way, but they sure know how to do it!

**Matt:** I do not teach any of the tech to my students. They use each other, YouTube videos, and tech blogs to figure out technical nuances.

How do you prepare for change itself? This book is designed to answer that question fully and comprehensively—to give you a plethora of activities and intellectual pathways that will allow you to prepare students for most anything that the world may throw at them, within the current curricular standards to which you have to teach.

But for the student, it's a slightly different story. That uncertainty about their future, that unpredictability about their personal professional trajectories, has ramifications. Regarding adolescent identity, the American Psychological Association (APA) notes the following: "Identity refers to more than just how adolescents see themselves right now; it also includes what has been termed the 'possible self'—what individuals might become and who they would like to become (Markus and Nurius, 1986)" (APA 2002, 15).

## The Quest for Possible Selves

Think back on your own personal and professional narrative. At what age did you start to land on the notion that you wanted to be in education? That you wanted to work with youth? Perhaps there were detours along the way before your current passion came into focus. What the APA is suggesting is that this way of thinking—the ability to imagine your future, your possible self—is essential to your development. I do some work with refugees, and this concept of the possible self comes up again and again. Why? Because many refugees simply can't imagine a possible self (see Figure 1–2); they can't look ahead five years and aim to land at this or that spot in society.

---

**Figure 1–2**

I work with a small team of refugees in the Kakuma Refugee Camp in Western Kenya to create a radio drama called *Sawa Shabab*. This camp has been in place since 1992 and currently has around 180,000 refugees. The refugees there are, at the moment of this writing, mostly South Sudanese and Somalian. I asked my thirty-two-year-old coworker, Clement, who is a South Sudanese refugee living in Kakuma, to share his ideas and experience about one's possible self. Here is Clement's answer:

> Now to your question of whether I/we have a sense of "Possible self." Just from a general refugee perspective, it is a *yes* and *no* situation.
>
> 1. It is a *yes* because a lot of Refugees youths are in the camp for different reasons. Most young folks here in the camp are desperately looking for opportunities to better themselves in the future. Scholarship opportunities, acquiring job experience in the camp, free affordable education, free pieces of training from agencies in the camp—all these are for them to become independent back in their country of origin, and this is where they visualize themselves in 3–5 years. So, a lot of youths in the camp definitely have a "possible self" mindset to

becoming something in the future. All the learning opportunities the refugees land here is for them to be better when they go back to their country of origin where they will get a job that pays well.

2. It is a *no* because a lot of youths have completely lost their hopes for their future because nothing seems to work out for them. They have lived here for more than twenty years, go back to South Sudan, come back to the Refugee camp and nothing seems to work out for them. So, these sections of people end up getting depressed and traumatized by their life experiences. When we were piloting our proposed survey the other day, there was a word that one of the Facilitators noted and he said it was a sensitive word to some refugee youths. The word was "hope." He said some youths might get very offended when asked if they have hopes in their future. It is a complicated situation because some youths in the camp are not able to foresee themselves in 2–3 years. Some have stayed in the camp for five years and never got any job or even invited for an interview. This has caused them to lose hope in everything in the camp.

3. As for me, I want to see myself acquire a college degree or diploma and run a business between 5–10 years from now. These goals can be affected by unpredictable circumstances whether you are a refugee or not a refugee. This set of goals requires total commitment and dedication to achieve them. As a refugee, you can set goals and try your best to achieve them—but in the blink of an eye, you can kiss goodbye to all your goals. The things you need to support your goals could be out of sight and that can easily drain hope out of you. I remember in 2010, I had a good job, and I had planned in three years, I would buy a plot in Juba South Sudan, in July 2013. We waited for land to be demarcated and get tokens for the plots. They delayed it up to December 15, 2013. That is when the war broke out and that plan got disrupted. We came here to Kakuma.

   To achieve what you need in a certain time frame you have to be strong in every circumstance and just pick yourself up, roll the sleeves, get going.

---

That narrative poignantly paints a portrait of the battleground between hope and despair for displaced persons. You may have students that are displaced persons or resettled refugees who struggle with imagining a possible self. But as I have noted, this need for imagining a possible self is universal and it is being compromised for all students, no matter their background or history.

The future is shifting at a new warp speed, which makes it really hard to bring it into focus. And if you can't quite picture your possible self—if the tools are not present to help you shape this personal and professional trajectory—then, as the APA suggests, identity development can suffer. Heather Sinclair, a seventh-grade science teacher, puts it this way:

> "We have this expectation that we will do some sort of workplace readiness for our students and it's sort of become this running joke that we are preparing them for jobs that don't exist yet. And we are! We probably are. . . . There is no way to predict the kind of world that they are going to live in. . . . With the growth of information sharing and the shifts in the way that technology and engineering in particular are impacting the world, I absolutely agree that we are preparing them for not only an unpredictable world, but a world in which unpredictability is the only predictable thing."

The good news: There are answers. Many, many answers. And answers that don't reek of compromise but instead aim for new understandings of knowledge, narrative and insightful perspectives. Our culture of omnipresent change is not a barrier, but a brand-new and welcome opening to make the educational process fun, engaging, challenging, and deeply rewarding. That's what this book is about.

There are four different pathways into digital storytelling in the classroom that we will investigate.

1. **Skills, Skills, Skills:** We'll begin with a focus on the skills that digital storytelling demands of the students—skills that are in high demand for success in a world characterized by change.
2. **Process, Process, Process:** Process is the focal point of the second pathway. We will dive into the playful and deep waters that characterize the journey from topic to finished product and the inherent educational value of that journey.
3. **Story, Story, Story:** There is a lot of fun to unearth here in our exploration of the elements of story and the continually expanding impact of storytelling in our society.
4. **Practice, Practice, Practice:** Practicing marks our final turn of events, as we go through a variety of options for integrating this project-based approach into your classroom.

Supporting these four pathways is a wide spectrum of projects, large and small. Inside of each chapter there are numerous in-class activities that are designed to take up one or two classes. Then each chapter concludes with three projects that are designed to be completed over the course of one or three weeks. The book concludes with three interdisciplinary digital storytelling projects designed to be produced by student teams over the course of three to four weeks.

In these projects and activities, the assumption is that the students will work in groups. It is my belief that the collaborative nature of digital storytelling increases the educational value exponentially. However, these projects can also be done by individual students as it is equally clear that not all students work well inside of group dynamics and that these collaborative structures can decimate educational value and impact. So, while the default position of this book is that this proposed work is best done in groups of three to four, it is up to you whether or not to apply that requirement across the range of your students.

The vast majority of these projects are part of an inventory of over 150 curriculum-driven, digital storytelling units that reside at Meridian Stories, the nonprofit I referenced at the start of this chapter. You can find these and other resources to support your digital storytelling classroom experience at www.meridianstories.com.

One more headline to note about your experience with this book. While this book has a sequential logic to it, you don't have to work through it sequentially. The design of this book does not adhere to a scope and sequence framework. Read the book. Scan the activities. Jump to the digital storytelling projects—here or on Meridian Stories—and dive in with your students, cherry-picking activities along the way or creating your own scope and sequence structure. In short, don't be overwhelmed by all the tributaries of exploration presented here.

This book has a simple ambition: to make digital storytelling normative in the upper-elementary, middle, and high school classroom. I want to take you on an investigative journey into the deeply engaging world of digital story creation so that you can jump onto the frontier of preparing your students for the uncertainties of the world . . . with certainty.

Let's get started.

CHAPTER TWO

# Preparing Youth for a Culture of Omnipresent Change

We left off Chapter 1 on a small cliff-hanger: How do we prepare our students for a future that is in a constant state of flux, a culture of omnipresent change?

The answer lies in a focus on what are commonly known as twenty-first-century skills: creativity, critical thinking, communication, and collaboration, to name just a few.

Margaret Heffernan, CEO, author of five books, radio dramatist, and entrepreneur, gave a TED talk in 2019 titled, "The Human Skills We Need in an Unpredictable World." In that talk she remarked:

> Preparedness, coalition building, imagination, experiments, bravery: in an unpredictable age these are tremendous sources of resilience and strength. They aren't efficient. But they give us limitless capacity for adaptation, variation, and invention. And the less we know about the future, the more we are going to need these tremendous sources of human, messy, unpredictable skills.

Who else is trying to corral the future? Some of the biggest corporations in the world. Amazon, for example, looks for applicants who have "demonstrated curiosity and . . . have solved a problem" (Umoh 2017). At IDEO, a global design firm based in California, they look for storytelling: "We think about design as a conversation. Being a good storyteller helps you keep up your end of the dialogue" (Zhou 2017). The company Indeed, which lays claim to being "the #1 job site in the world with over 250 million unique visitors every month," lists fourteen qualities that should be highlighted in your résumé, including teamwork, determination, dependability, flexibility, and problem-solving (Indeed Editorial Team 2021).

There are many more examples from corporations and universities—at Brown University (n.d.), "intellectual curiosity, individual perspectives and creativity" top the list—and they all point toward the same thing: in a culture of omnipresent change, where students will be more challenged than ever to craft their possible selves, the kinds of skills we need to be focusing on include creativity, collaboration, bravery (fascinating, that one!), storytelling, flexibility, problem-solving, and imagination.

However, to many, the phrase *twenty-first-century skills* feels archaic and no longer reflective of the urgency with which we need to teach these skills. To me, it also feels confining, as if the list were all settled upon and we just needed to check the boxes. The list is not set. The skills are additive with time and with change. Some people use the phrase *life skills*, *futures skills*, or *essential skills*. In professional circles they are often referred to as *soft skills* . . . which makes my temperature rise a few degrees. I prefer to borrow Margaret Heffernan's phrase: *human skills*. The term implies universal accessibility, open-endedness, optimism, and, in the face of technology's continued rise, a certain balance of power . . . in favor of our biological selves!

## Human Skills: The Grist of Digital Storytelling

Human skills are the traits that students need to enter a workplace that is in constant motion. Human skills are about training the mind to take calculated risks, look for patterns, and transpose failure into opportunity. They are about listening, delegating, empathizing, and imagining. You can draw up this list any way you want, setting priorities based on your community and your personal values system. But either way, the explicit work on these skill sets begins in the classroom.

In the end, we are talking about ways of thinking and interacting with the world. We are talking about curating a student's identity from operating in a narrow, finite sense of self to an infinite sense of self. Not pie-in-the-sky infinite. No. We are talking I-can-handle-most-things-that-come-my-way infinite. Open-ended thinking.

## What Is the Most Important Human Skill to Teach?

**Tamiko:** Oh, my goodness. I have not given that complete thought because I just wrap everything up together. I think resiliency is the most important. I think teaching our students to fail forward. 'Cause when you step, you fail forward, when you get up, you may be bruised, but you are two steps forward rather than falling back. I think that resiliency builds trust; it builds your own self-confidence; it builds empathy; it builds kindness; it builds hope.

**Bill:** The biggest skill across subjects that I teach is the ability to take perspectives, the ability to take empathy for people whose experiences might differ from their own. . . . Perspective taking . . . an ability to see things through different lenses, whether that be class lenses or racial lenses or cultural lenses—I think that's superimportant for kids to consider how the world can look different through different sets of lenses.

**Emily:** I think the most important skill set is the process of problem-solving. Almost everything is problem-solving. What are you going to have for dinner? That's a problem. How do you solve this math problem? Well, what knowledge do you have and how are you going to apply it? Why was there some battle? It's all the same thing of identifying the issue, coming up with your resources, and proposing some sort of solution.

**Heather:** I have two. One is going to be informational gathering and prioritizing. What do you need to know; how true is it; how do I prioritize information from the world around me? And the other one is going to be comfort in change. Some sort of flexibility. And that really does link to creativity. What is my role? How is my role going to change? What is that going to mean moving forward? Those are two incredibly broad skills, but I would say that informational prioritizing and flexibility in the way that you handle change.

**Andrea:** You know, when we think about most of our conversations, it's facial expressions and body language. So teaching them how to communicate effectively on a computer when you don't have all of those things.

**Alyssa:** Collaboration is my biggest thing because middle schoolers are so hard; they're always worried about how other people would view them, so that's why I always focus on collaboration. [Next], adaptability, for sure. That's an important life skill in general; not everything's going to go your way, or when something goes wrong, how do you fix it, how do you adapt, how do you move on? And then, listening skills because I feel like in middle school it just goes in one ear and out the other and sometimes you need to read between the lines when you're social with other students or your friends. You know, your teachers don't just talk for nothing. [*A beat later*] . . . Maybe I would change my answer to time management—being able to produce the whole project by the due date. Yes, time management.

**Ell:** Teamwork. They are kind of still figuring out what their strengths are, and in some cases, they are making those discoveries in the course of working on the (digital storytelling) challenge. I would say that . . . I don't know if it would be the teamwork. This is a hard question. I think critical thinking is the most important. And, creativity, but that is my own preference, but it's so necessary, and it's not happening enough, and I love it.

Morgan Cuthbert, a seventh-grade science teacher, sums it up this way:





> **"You have to look at something bigger than just your classroom. I always look at our kids and say, 'Are we making them successful to make their own decisions or are we specifically driving them to one content area?' I think we have to make them successful to look at any problem that's out there."**

"Any problem that's out there." That's human skills. For students to imagine and then drive toward their possible selves in a culture of omnipresent change, they need this tool kit of human skills. As people, this is what we want for ourselves. As teachers, this is what we want for our students.

ACTIVITY

## Human Skills Survey

A simple, short, and deeply instructive activity is to survey your students on these human skills. The idea isn't to come up with a definitive list. The debate of whether resiliency is more important than empathy is, in my view, a pointless one. They are both superimportant. I tend to believe that creativity is the number one human skill. *Forbes Magazine* published a widely circulated list of skills necessary to succeed in 2020, and it begins with complex problem-solving, goes through people management, and bottoms out at service management (Beckford 2018).

Everyone has their priorities.

What *you* want to know is which human skills your kids think are the most important and which are the hardest. This will tell you what they want from you in terms of projects and processes throughout the year, and what they perceive are the hardest skills to master. Equally as important, this will raise awareness of these human skills to your students; it will put these terms and skill sets on their radar.

Administer the Student Questionnaire shown in Figure 2–1, giving the students fifteen or twenty minutes to fill it out. If you do this at the start of your year or semester, you will have a nuanced portrait of how your students are thinking; of their perceived obstacles while growing up amid a culture of omnipresent change; and of how your students are glimpsing their possible selves.

Figure 2–1

## Student Questionnaire

Prioritize this list of Human Skills by numbering your top five skills in the order of importance to you. Then add one of your own, if you notice that something is missing.

| | | |
|---|---|---|
| Resiliency | Collaboration | Digital Literacy |
| Creativity | Empathy | Problem-Solving |
| Critical Thinking | Flexibility and Adaptability | Independent Initiative |
| Presentational Skills and Public Speaking | Perseverance and Grit | Leadership |
| Effective Communication | Intellectual Curiosity | Decision-Making |
| Add your own: | | |

1. Please write two to four sentences explaining your first two choices: why do you believe those skills are the most important for your current and future self?
2. Which of the above human skills do you think are the hardest, for you, to master and why? Please answer in two to four sentences.

I want to share with you a few interesting and thoughtful results from one middle school classroom of twenty-six students who responded to this survey.

- Creativity was by far and away the human skill that was most important to these youth, with eleven citing it as the number one skill and eighteen, or just under 70 percent, ranking creativity in their top five human skills.
- Problem-solving and intellectual curiosity followed in terms of the number of times they were cited in the top five, at 57 percent and 46 percent, respectively.

- Digital literacy was not mentioned once as an important human skill. Why? I can only speculate that either (1) this was a skill over which they believed that they had control and was not one that they believed their teacher could help them master or (2) this skill didn't belong in this list: it was perceived as more of a hard skill than a soft skill and therefore wasn't relevant to this activity.
- When asked which of these human skills were the hardest to master, seven cited presentational skills and public speaking, and six cited decision-making, with the remaining thirteen students spread out over the rest of the skills. Here are some of their explanations:
    - "I think public speaking because I get stressed and mess up my words. Also, my head fills up with thoughts."
    - "I get nervous and flustered."
    - "Trying to speak without repeating or saying 'Uh' a lot is hard."
    - "I think that decision-making is the hardest because sometimes I overthink about decisions and sometimes I underthink."
    - "Decision making is very hard for me. I think it's hard for me because I wonder later, 'What if I had done that instead?'"
    - "Presentational skills are some of the hardest for me along with decision making, as I am very indecisive and I also struggle with confidence. Both of these skills will serve me well once I can master them."

As a result of this data, if I were their teacher, I would approach the year by:

- emphasizing public-speaking skills—creating situations that would require them to present their work to the class and, possibly, a broader public;
- creating an awareness about decision-making—making those internal mental processes more external—and creating some time to discuss some of the broad parameters around how to make good decisions; and
- focusing on the role of creativity in all of the projects, whether they demanded explicit or implicit creative solutions, while tying that in with fostering intellectual curiosity because I think the one is connected to the other.

Additionally, I would pay attention to the needs of individual students—their perceived strengths and fears as articulated in their choices and comments—and use that information to personalize their course of study.

You know what delivers human skills in spades *while* probing deep curricular content *and* issues of identity development (we're talking possible selves)? Digital storytelling. Here's why.

- Digital stories are team-based efforts. Therefore, they are collaborative, which includes practicing skills such as people management, delegation, leadership, and coordinating with others.
- Digital stories are scripted and often character-driven. Therefore, they require creativity and imagination.
- Digital stories are composed of many small decisions about research, narrative structure, look, and sound. Therefore, they invite problem-solving, decision-making, and critical thinking.
- Digital stories require students to research content and tell their own story about that content. Therefore, they require evidence-based reasoning and are empowering.
- Digital stories are designed to be shared with an audience of more than just one (you, the teacher). Therefore, they invite presentational skills.

These are all essential human skills that allow students to engage authentically with curricular content. Digital storytelling is a win-win.

## Two New Human Skills: Visual and Auditory Cognizance

To tell a good story, you need a command of words, in all their complexity. Words are the primary ingredient of storytelling. To tell a good *digital* story, you need command of a whole lot more. And this is where the fun begins.

The coolest quality about digital storytelling is the myriad tools at one's disposal to effectively communicate: sound, imagery, words, and music. When you apply all of these elements to a narrative about a poem or a physical force, a treaty or a planet, the content jumps off the page and into the world of sound and moving imagery, vocal language and music. It's living content. You don't rely on the reader to bring the story to life, as in a book. *You*—the creator—bring it to life. And *that* is a critical part of the empowering experience of digital storytelling: ownership.

Sound, imagery, words, and music: these are the crossover elements between real life and digital life. In real life, they are laid out all around you, organized and random, shaping your every second. In digital life, they are tools that allow you to create stories for others to experience. Learning how to use sound to shape the narrative experience; learning how to use music to craft the emotional trajectory of the narrative; learning how to use words as active visual components and not just receptacles of meaning; and learning how imagery communicates, manipulates, evokes, horrifies, and soothes are all vital skills to effectively communicate and have your voice heard in this digital age. These are relatively new skills to add to the human skills inventory. For the sake of this book, I will refer to them as skills of visual and auditory cognizance.

If students can shift from being relatively passive receptors of these sensory elements to being hyperaware of them—to be on the lookout for beauty; to spot the trumpet riff in that song; to hear the loon call; and to comment upon a strange and funny-sounding word when they come across it (*conundrum* springs to mind)—then, in my mind, they will have surpassed any standards set out by external educational forces.

Digital storytelling is a true crossover experience between our biological and digital worlds. The more you are aware of and engage with the way the world communicates to you—through sound, imagery, words, and music—the better able you are to tap into these tools to communicate effectively with the world, both in real life and digitally.

Sound, imagery, words, and music: when you have to layer them together, the process can be complex. Similarly, when you have to layer them together, the process can be exciting. Complex *and* exciting: this is what we want for our students.

# Spirited Activities for the Classroom

What follows are ideas and activities that are designed to creatively explore and interrogate the component parts of visual and auditory cognizance: sound, imagery, words, and music.

## Sound

Two of my favorite academic quotes of all time come from *Orality and Literacy: The Technologizing of the Word*, by Walter Ong (1982), a book and author whom I introduced in Chapter 1:

> **In a primary oral culture, where the word has its existence only in sound . . . the phenomenology of sound enters deeply into human beings' feel for existence, as processed by the spoken word. (72)**

> **Sight isolates, sound incorporates. Whereas sight situates the observer outside what he views, at a distance, sound pours into the hearer.** (71)

These quotes have always pointed to the strength and beauty of the invisible sense: sound. Think about it. If music is too loud, you can't think. If you are at a concert surrounded by music that moves you, you don't want to think; you just move. Look at those phrases: "sounds enter deeply in human beings' feel for existence" and "sound pours into the hearer." It's true: it's a sensory experience that seeps into us—and reduces our power to control ourselves and think rationally.

Sound is, in my view, the key distinguishing element to any digital story. It is sound that is often in the lead in controlling the experience of the viewer—whether they know it or not.

There are four different kinds of sounds in digital storytelling of which to be aware.

## Ambient Sound

Did you know that at the end of every scene shot for a movie, they tell everyone to be quiet and they record one minute of "room tone," or ambient sound? Why? Because silence sounds differently in different spaces. Just consider the silence of an empty classroom versus the silence of a small, closed-door conference room versus the silence of a soaring church space. Producers need these room tones to lay under scenes taking place in that room.

Whatever story students are telling, have them consider laying down an ambient track. This can be the quiet room tone, as previously mentioned, or the low hush of conversations at a café; the waiting room of a dentist's office; or the blow-dryers and faucets at a salon. Rooms "speak," whether deliberately or not.

ACTIVITY

### Ambient Soundtracks

Have the students collect a few samples of ambient sound around your school and see if their classmates can tell where each recording has taken place. Here is one way to do this.

- Before class, create a list of distinct places in your school. I suggest keeping this limited to interior spaces like the library, gym, cafeteria, and hallway. Write these places on small slips of paper, fold them, and place them in a container, like a shoebox or a hat.
- Form your class into small groups of two or three. Have each group select a place from the box and keep their place a secret from the others. Have them

go to that place to record thirty seconds of ambient sound. They can do this on their phones, as most will have an audio recording app or can use a video recording app to capture the sound.

- After all the groups come back, ask Group A to play their soundtrack for the class, and have Group B guess the location, aloud. Then have Group B play their soundtrack and Group C guess. And around it goes.

Some of the answers will be obvious. But in the quieter places, one has to listen really hard to try to imagine the shape of the room that is crafting that "quiet." A classroom or the auditorium when no one is there. At the end of this exercise, ask if anyone heard something that they had never noticed before. The thrust of this activity is to sensitize the students to the sounds that they hear, but may not acknowledge, around them. You are building their auditory cognizance.

## Natural Sound

When was the last time you sat in an empty park, the woods, by the beach, or in a field and closed your eyes and just listened? Nothing happens at first. And then, slowly, sounds reveal themselves to you. The wind, the squirrel, the wren, the distant highway, the dog bark, the basketball bouncing, and so on.

While the phrase *ambient sound* can apply to outdoor spaces as well, it is generally reserved for how interior walls, carpeting, and the actions and voices of people shape sound. With *natural sounds*, I am referring to sounds that emanate outside: both man-made and natural.

ACTIVITY

### Sound Stories of Place

Here is an activity that I recommend students do after school, which will give them the freedom to choose a location that is not necessarily near or on school grounds.

- In class, each student identifies an exterior place that interests them in terms of what sounds they might hear. It could be a backyard, a town park, a balcony, a gas station, the woods, a sidewalk bench, the shore of a lake or sea or river—it's up to them.

- Each student should plan to spend fifteen minutes in that place with a notebook in hand—or a laptop—writing all the sounds that they hear over the course of those fifteen minutes. They can set a timer on their phone.
- They should try not to talk during this period: all of their focus is on listening, especially for sounds that slowly make their presence known through time and concentration, like a distant plane—sounds that were not noticeable at first.
- At the end of the fifteen minutes, they write one sentence designed to capture the essence of the world that the student heard during that fifteen-minute stretch. A descriptive statement of place as defined by what they heard.
- Back in class the next day, let the students take the first ten minutes of class to write their sounds and summary statements on the board or easel pads so that everyone can see their work.
- As the teacher, take a step back and look at all the sounds. Here are a few leading questions to consider asking the class:
    - → In any given grouping of sounds, is there a story to be invented, on the spot?
    - → Look at the summary statements. Does the audio conjure up whole, fully imagined places?
    - → What was the experience of just listening? Soothing and peaceful? Tense and anxious? Emotional?
    - → Does that location, after this experience, have a fuller dimension or meaning for you?
    - → What specific sounds would you be sure to include in a digital story that took place in or near that kind of location?

The overall goal is to increase students' auditory cognizance—to increase their awareness of sound as a proactive sense that shapes place, story, and emotional states of being—so that they can use these sounds effectively as storytelling tools.

## Foley Sound

Arguably the most enjoyable piece of sound production is becoming a "Foley artist": a creator of sound effects. For example, what if your mic didn't pick up the sound of footsteps on gravel *and* you don't have gravel lying around to help rerecord that sound? What do you do? Experiment! You could place potato chips in a tray and record crunching them with your hand. Does that sound like crunching gravel? Probably not. What else might replicate the sound of gravel? That's the problem that needs to be solved and that's what professional Foley artists do:





- Look at the video footage.
- Identify the missing sound—it could simply be the ruffling of clothing as two characters hug.
- Find a way to recreate that sound (the classic example is to create the sounds of a horse trotting with coconut shells).
- And finally, match the sound to the picture in the sound mix.

Students can do this for audio stories and podcasts as well.

ACTIVITY

## Sound Creativity: Foley Bursts

Invite your students to be Foley artists by allowing them to play with everyday items in order to create sound effects. Following is a list of items that you can bring to class that will get you started, but feel free to augment this list with anything that can help produce a sound. Or ask the students to bring in three everyday items that they think will contribute to creating a unique sound.

- **flyswatter**
- **hand fan**
- **bowl of gravel**
- **bowl of potato chips (or five small bags of chips)**
- **broom**
- **pinecone**
- **rubber gloves**
- **deck of cards**
- **newspaper, tissue paper, or cellophane**
- **drumsticks**
- **baseball mitt**
- **bowl of marbles**
- **bowl of pennies**
- **jackets hanging about**
- **guitar or stringed instrument**
- **metal mixing bowl**

Working in pairs, students spend fifteen minutes creating two specific sounds by combining or manipulating the props you brought in. Then they write a short moment—just two or three sentences designed to capture a dramatic moment or simple everyday transactions like getting bottled water at a vending machine—that will be read out loud by one of the students while the two sound effects are performed by the second student. Your students can either locate a sound and create an action around it or come up with the action first and look to create the sound.

Examples of moments could include people eating together and spilling something; someone bumping into someone else; opening a window and hearing a mysterious sound; buying a soft drink and paying with change; or striking something hard (treasure?) while digging in dirt or sand.

Examples of sounds effects include creaky doors opening; cash being counted; a campfire; birds flapping their wings; people scuffling; footsteps on wood, gravel, pavement, grass, or snow; an arrow passing by the ear; chewing loudly; or that *thunk* sound you hear when you try to push through a subway turnstile that doesn't turn!

In the end, students present their short audio scenes (and perhaps the audience closes their eyes while listening). As a result, the opportunity to actually manufacture sound is now a viable option for your students in their digital storytelling. Repositioning a blazing campfire as the crinkling of cellophane paper is another part of increasing their auditory cognizance.

In terms of human skills, this activity targets presentational skills, creativity, problem-solving, iterative thinking, and collaboration.

## Prerecorded Sound Effects

Prerecorded sound effects can be natural sounds, like bird sounds added to a park scene to increase the ambience, but they can also be unnatural, like a rim shot or a trombone slide or a *thwack*! These sounds are added to help create tone, as in comedies, satires, and parodies. They help guide the viewer as to the intended effect you want from a scene. Libraries of royalty-free sound effects abound on the internet and can often be useful to provide students with sounds that they had never even considered.

# Imagery

How do you teach students to write using imagery? Digital stories don't have syntax or grammar like text-based writing does. The structure and infrastructure of digital storytelling almost solely lie with the logic of the storyteller, and not on a set of external rules with verbs and nouns, commas and paragraphs. In other words, there is no formal grammar to digital storytelling; images don't have to be placed in a syntactically acceptable order to make sense. The flow from one image to the next is determined by the logic of the narrative, not grammar. To compound matters, images lack the precision of meaning that words do. The word *couch* has a very clear meaning. But a picture of just a couch, in an empty room, can mean despair, loneliness, silence, relaxation, abandonment, frugality: there are infinite interpretations. So, as a teacher, how do you help the students structure a cohesive narrative using imagery?

I have not yet found a clear answer. The best we can do is to try to understand the nature of the beast and communicate with students the range and depth of meaning of a single image.

One way to go about this is to compare imagery to text. English text works with twenty-six symbols. Done deal. And while I could go on about the miracle that this is—that the vast English language can be captured in its infinite breadth by twenty-six symbols—this moment isn't about text. Imagery (and in this discussion, moving imagery is always included), on the other hand, is composed of a range of visual options. A short list includes:

- graphics
- watercolor images
- animation (or CGI)
- clay animation
- original or existing video
- data visualization
- doodles
- green screen
- woodprints
- oil painting
- photos (color or black-and-white)

This is important because the choice of each visual option connotes something different. Take that same couch. An animated frame of a couch differs from a photo of a couch in a catalog, which differs from a black-and-white charcoal drawing of a couch. All three refer to different experiences—different narratives, as it were.

Here are some simple ideas to begin to deepen an awareness among your students about (1) how to understand the way imagery communicates and (2) how to understand how to use imagery effectively in storytelling.

Once you and your class have explored the explosive range of meaning inside a given image, then you can assume that the students will bring that heightened awareness to their own digital storytelling work.

## Image Captions

As a way to open the door to how a single image can evoke a wide array of interpretations, focus on captioning: the attempt to capture the image in words. Is there a work of public art or a mural near where you live, historical or recently created? Think of all the people who witness this imagery. Then consider this: do you believe that what you see is similar to what others see? What are the odds that your caption would match a random selection of captions of others who are looking at the same piece? I think the odds are slim, and an activity that opens that awareness, that creates a visceral experience into the variability of perspective that images invoke, is going to be productive. Try this.

*The New Yorker* magazine has a weekly cartoon caption contest that is free. *The New Yorker* supplies the cartoon and you supply the caption. They pick three finalists and you vote on the funniest. Consider involving your class in this contest for a month.

ACTIVITY

## Captioning Images: Pictures Versus Words

- Choose two or three images that relate to the topic you are teaching. Think political cartoons, memes (captions removed), masterpiece drawings (ancient and modern), data visualizations and diagrams, period photographs, portraits, or Google Earth images. Think literal and figurative imagery.
- Ask the students to work in teams to develop a title, caption, or short description of the images, like you might see in a museum.
- Project each image on a screen in front of the class and have the students write their captions around that image, on a board or an easel.
- Compare and contrast their answers.

This activity is not only a good one to expose the myriad ways in which imagery communicates but also a great catalyst for debates about your content. Also note how a caption or title can reframe the meaning of an image. For a second round in the last five minutes of class, choose one of the images and have the students turn the image into a meme.

## Picture Time Lines

Text and images function in different ways. There are things each does well—and things each doesn't do well. For the scientific process, the text may bring us right to the critical moment of each part of the sequence, whereas the image may leave out a lot of information. For character arcs, the images may communicate more substance than the written text. And vice versa for both subjects.

In the end, you want to bring out how each medium communicates differently while pointing to the communicative strengths of imagery, in particular. And this is particularly important when trying to balance textual literacy and digital literacy projects in your classroom.

In this activity you want to explore the differences between how imagery and text communicate both information and story. As a warm-up, consider this: Contrast two lines of biographical information about Maya Angelou against a picture of her, with a short caption of where and when it was taken. So, two lines written, say, on a board to the far left of your classroom, and a picture projected or hung, far right. Which experience of Maya Angelou has more impact? Which experience communicates the most to the students or makes them want to know more?

ACTIVITY

## A Story in Three Pictures

- You assign three points in a sequence you are studying—a story or character arc, a scientific process, a historical event. The points could be very specific (points in a sequence that you have identified as critically important) or general (beginning, middle, and end).
- Half the groups represent those three points in text, writing two sentences per point.
- The other half represent these moments in images. Limit this to one or two images—found or created—per moment. They also get to create captions for their images, up to eight words each.
- For this activity, there are no video or Prezi-like presentations: this is about static imagery.
- Pick two groups from each half and have them visually (no talking) showcase their work. Have the class compare and contrast the information and stories being told.

Like the previous activity, this is designed to be another creative launching pad for a discussion about content. For our purposes here, the idea is not to see which medium communicates more effectively, but to see how each medium communicates differently, enriching the overall narrative.

## Image Sequencing: The Photo-Essay

Imagine allowing your students the chance to tell a wordless story about August Wilson's life or the life cycle of a bee or a decade in your local town, using just eight images. No words, except, if desired, the who, when, and where: Rosalind Franklin–1954–London. Ruminate on this idea for a beat. My first concern would be, how would students tell an accurate story without words? My second thought is, is accuracy the prevailing criterion for an engaging and educationally substantive narrative? In my view, the answer is no. It is a criterion, but perhaps not the dominant one. And having students work through the process of figuring that out—of constructing a story that needs to clearly and effectively communicate educational content without the tools (words) on which they have mostly relied up to now—is educational gold unto itself.

Susan Sontag, the author of the seminal text on the subject of photo-essays, *On Photography*, has this nugget to share: "Photographed images do not seem to be statements about the world so much as pieces of it, miniatures of reality that anyone can make or acquire" (1977, 2). Eight "miniatures of reality" that, when placed together, communicate a narrative. Here's how that might work.

ACTIVITY

## A Story in Eight Pictures: Getting Personal

- Either you assign the topic based on what you are studying, you provide a range of topics from which to choose (e.g., Black authors of the twentieth century; endangered species; Nobel Peace Prize winners), or students pick their own topics. But no matter the parameters, this activity—this story—is about a person or group of people. It's a story not about what this person did so much as who this person is. That's the goal: to humanize this historical, literary, scientific, or artistic person or group.
- In groups of two or three, students spend a few class periods researching their subject. Have your students use primary and secondary sources, print and imagery, to try to piece together what in this person's life made them who they are or were.
- Groups create a written outline of that story and then select the images, up to eight.
- Once the images are selected, plan to devote two classes to putting together presentations. It's up to you if you will allow students to add captions—say, up to ten words per picture—or keep it wordless, or add music and sound effects.
    - → In this presentational form, I recommend letting the students choose the format—a video, a Prezi or other fluid form of singular frame sequencing, or printed pictures tacked to a wall. They can make it simple or elaborate; they can control the whole experience or let the viewer control it by going through the images at their own pace, in their own time. Let the students play with and make decisions about these digital options.
- As a culmination of the unit, students present their stories.

In discussing the stories, you can dig into the order of the images. Does the chosen order move the narrative along in a linear fashion? Or is it more of a montage effect whereby the images create an impression more than a story? What about the pacing with which they deliver the images? Is it evenly paced, or do they purposefully linger on one image and then shoot through the next few? Are there visual patterns to these choices, such as repeating color schemes or settings? Is there a movement between close-ups and wide shots that indicates a dialogue between shots?

Most importantly, what did the students get from the experience of researching and telling a story in this fashion? Was it harder than a traditional paper, easier, or just different? And if just different, how? Finally, what did the students learn from viewing and discussing a person of interest through the lens of these eight images?

My own personal view of this activity is that while a paper on the person of interest may communicate more factual information in an organized way, it is generally a finite educational experience. But a photo-essay is a launching pad for some intellectual discussion and exploration. That is one of the distinctions of the extensive use of imagery in the classroom: it provokes discussion.

In the end, we all live in a visual world. But our digital native students live in a hyper-visual world; one source cited in Business Insider estimated that people would take one hundred billion more photos in 2017 than they did in 2016 (Cakebread 2017). Who is looking, sharing, meming, and tagging the vast majority of those pictures?

Your students.

One. Hundred. Billion.

*More* . . . in a single year.

Digging into the nuanced power of effective visual communication—visual cognizance—is clearly a rising human skill that will help your students to communicate effectively inside of the digital universe that envelops them, now . . . and in the future.

## Words

Let's cut right to the chase with this component: words are not second-class citizens in digital storytelling. Nope. The mandate here: bring words to visual life. They are, after all, composed of visual symbols. They are visual.

I used to work on a show for PBS called *Ghostwriter*. We are talking the early nineties, although the series was recently resurrected with a new cast for Apple TV+. The show was funded to be a "literacy show" targeting eight- to twelve-year-olds. OK. So, in the creative brainstorming phase, the producers and writers had this conundrum: How would they create a "literacy show" that was designed to encourage kids to enjoy reading and writing . . . for television? How do you make words the star of the show?

The answer was to create, as the central character, a ghost who had no voice or physical presence but existed only in the printed (or in this case, animated) word to help other characters solve a mystery. So, in order to understand the story at key moments in the mystery, you, as the viewer, had to *read* this character.

This was a brilliant solution. Central character as language itself. And it worked.

## Vivifying Language

Here's the opportunity: in digital storytelling you can help to make language come alive in ways that are novel and surprising. That is, I would argue, of huge value: releasing words from the white page and computer screen and then allowing them to flourish as both designed symbols and cool avatars of meaning. Here are some ways students can integrate language into their digital stories:

- Make words actual characters in the story.
- Use color and font and size to give them figurative vocal cords.
- Add music and sound effects to give words movement . . . down a spiraled pathway or up a steep incline, perhaps.
- Play around with texting, a still evolving incarnation of writing that is yet another indication that language and writing are *alive*. Texting, as we all well know, is writing that exists within a loosely fluid set of rules. *Use it*. Tell stories in it.

The thrust here: digital storytelling allows kids to *play* with language. It's not just sentence plus sentence plus sentence equals paragraph. Words can take on their own life when students get to craft their use in a visual and aural setting.

This is your challenge as the teacher in this digital storytelling area: to help kids make written text—at various moments—the star of their digital stories by emphasizing the many ways words can be visualized where both the word itself and the inherent meaning can move the narrative forward. You want students to experience language as playful and alive and challenging. The activity Essay Analysis: Taking Control! on page 43 is one project that exemplifies this concept of bringing language to life visually while taking a deep dive into curricular content.

ACTIVITY

## Fun with Vocabulary: Short Audio Stories About Words

This is an overnight vocabulary activity that can be used whether you are teaching scientific terms or straight-up language arts vocabulary. Break your classroom into pairs. Give each pair two challenging words, for example, *discombobulate* and *anomaly*. Have them create a sixty-second audio monologue or dialogue (that is recorded on their computer or smartphone) in which they have to use each word twice, and every time they say the words, there is an echo effect or something to bring attention to those words and the context in which they are used. You do that, and words—hard words—become fun because the students get to play with them. And they will never forget them nor what they mean. This is a short assignment where the creative concept is shaped by a few select words, and then by how the students decide to produce those words. This can help students begin to reimagine their relationship to language and text.

# Music

In the late nineties there was a phenomenon called *The Dark Side of Oz*. A few of you out there know exactly what I am talking about. *The Dark Side of Oz* was a DVD that you could find at underground record and DVD stores that matched the soundtrack of Pink Floyd's *The Dark Side of the Moon* with MGM's *The Wizard of Oz* movie, stripped of its original soundtrack. While Pink Floyd has repeatedly denied that that album was created as an alternative soundtrack to the movie, the synchronicity between the score and the movie are, at moments, amazing. The point: seeing *The Wizard of Oz* scored with prog rock music changes the entire experience of the movie. The movie shifts from fairytale to a dark tale of human despair and capitalism gone astray, as moving into color isn't all that it's cracked up to be (the *cha-ching* from the song "Money" is the first thing heard as Dorothy steps into the Technicolor of Munchkinland).

## Playing with Soundtracks

Here's the headline about music: it is *the* vital tool to shape the tone and mood of the narrative experience. For me, tone refers to the comprehensive perspective of the storyteller, while mood refers to the shifting emotional dynamics within the story that help to establish our personal identification with the story. Mood shifts constantly, whereas tone tends to be established at the start and sustained throughout. Music establishes both and makes the argument for how tone and mood can be as important as character and plot in shaping our experience with the story being told.

The best way to illustrate this is to play a scene from TV or a movie and run different kinds of music underneath that scene.

In terms of our auditory cognizance, music is the aural bridge right to the emotional core of your audience. With just three stanzas of music, you can communicate whether or not the scene is tragic, funny, playful, tense, mysterious, sad, or callous.

ACTIVITY

## Music Is the Story

There is a YouTube video that takes a scene from the action series *Heroes* and repeats that same twenty-six-second scene twelve times, each with a different musical underscore. You can find this by searching "HEROES Season 2 - Big music test" in YouTube. It's a 2007 video, and the creator goes by the moniker of wlad33. The purpose is to show how music scoring changes our relationship to the scene each time.

- Watch this video with your students. Be aware that this short scene contains violence (in a cartoonish way).
- After each viewing, stop the video, and ask your class two questions:
    - → What is the tone of this scene?
    - → How are we meant to understand these characters?

Write the answers on the board after each viewing—some will overlap, as many of these musical choices tend toward the comic—and note how the music alone shaped how we were meant to experience that short scene.

# Digital Storytelling Projects

What follows are three classroom activities from what I call the Digital Incentive Series. They are designed to offer up an engaging approach to learning. These can be applied to history, English language arts, or STEAM classes—and by adding a digital layer, they make the learning and student engagement exponentially more powerful. In particular, these digital layers focus on the components of digital storytelling that we have been talking about: sound, music, words, and imagery. Each of these activities can take one or two classes, or one or two weeks, depending on how many of the digital options you want to pursue.

PROJECT

## Your Daily Score

**Language Arts:** identity and personal environmental exploration; audio cognizance; storytelling; human skills

**Digital Media:** audio recording and editing

**Time:** one to two weeks

# Your Daily Score

**Language Arts:** identity and personal environmental exploration; audio cognizance; story-telling; human skills

**Digital Media:** audio recording and editing

**Time:** one to two weeks

## Introduction

This activity challenges your students to create a short audio self-portrait without a word coming out of their mouths. It challenges them to work individually and shift into a high gear of audio awareness and to listen for the sounds that shape their daily existence. It's a day-in-the-life . . . in sounds. It begins on paper and in words.

## In the Classroom

- Have students take fifteen minutes to identify what they *think* are the ten key sounds in their daily life: the alarm clock; the bus pulling up; the principal over the loudspeaker; the basketballs bouncing; the piano; the video game sound; and so on. The word *key* is meant to be interpreted loosely. It could mean most memorable, most pervasive, or most significant and meaningful. It's up to the student.
  - → For this activity, students can include only one voice in this list and let's keep music off the list. Students can include music they play or create, but not music they listen to: this isn't about creating a playlist. Finally, consider asking them to include only sounds they hear without an earbud.
- Have the students take the rest of class time and an overnight to write a one-page daily self-portrait, bringing all ten identified sounds into the story. The format is meant to be very loose. The easiest narrative structure is a day-in-the-life, where students present sounds in chronological order. But they may end up grouping certain sounds—for example, sounds related to food or digital experiences—and the significance of those clusters of sounds. There is no right or wrong. It's students exploring how sounds relates to their evolving identity.
  - → After making his list and before they begin to outline their story, encourage them to really consider the sounds, shimmied free from associations with sports or school or being on the computer. Are they soft sounds? Abrasive? Sonorous? Hectic? Threatening? Soothing?
- Then ask students to voluntarily read aloud their one-page audio daily self-portraits. This gives the class a chance to hear how everyone else structured this open-ended narrative activity. Their narrative capacities will widen and students' understanding of their world, as observed through the ears and not the eyes, will be enhanced.

## Digital Incentive

- Thinking and writing about sounds is one thing. Actually going out and recording them is another. And that is the purpose of this digital incentive: bringing this one-page paper to life in audio. The first step can be as simple as that: take the work that the student has written up and use that as the basis for a thirty-second audio story. The student begins the story by stating their name and ends the story by concluding with their name. Their voice is not heard anywhere else.
- But if the purpose is partially to increase audio cognizance, try this: Have students find five–to–ten more sounds that were not in their original list. In other words, you are asking the students to spend a day actively listening to their life, as if they have stepped outside of their bodies and are shadowing themselves. If time permits, give them a couple of days to listen, take notes, and then record.
  - → At this point it's not about their key sounds as much as it is about sounds that shape their environment. Some of these sounds they may have not been aware of at all, but now they are. Crickets. The radiator. Honking cars. Phone notifications. The TV that is never turned off.
- In both of these variations, the final step is to construct some sort of narrative—some sort of cohesion—out of this collection of sounds. It's tough to do on paper and even tougher to do inside of a thirty-second audio story. You may want to cap it out at sixty seconds. And here's the fun part: our traditional sense of story now sort of falls apart. The students are now bound not by a beginning, middle, and end, but by how these sounds dialogue with each other and sound together as one. This is a hard story to plan ahead of time. It's only when the student hears it, that they can start moving things around; increasing and decreasing volume; sustaining some sounds—the calls of the seagulls or the fire engines' siren—and cutting off others; and playing with contrasts, as a way to communicate the various competing aural dynamics of their daily lives.

## Conclusion

Ironically, this is an eye-opening activity. To understand one's self through sound is to possibly open up a whole new portal into one's identity. Specifically, by actively observing outside of one's consciousness rather than probing inside the mind. It's a little counterintuitive (for middle and high schoolers) and wonderfully expansive. Equally as important, it opens up a new sensory portal to the world around them. And as stated numerous times in this chapter, a greater awareness of the soundtrack or score in your life leads to a richer use of sound in your digital storytelling.

PROJECT

# "I Am From" Poem

**Language Arts:** personal memoir; poetry; public speaking; human skills
**Digital Media:** short, singular or montage video
**Time:** one to two weeks

## Introduction

There is a teen series, of which I was a Co-Executive Producer, that was produced in Iraq from 2010-2013 called *Salam Shabab* ("Peace Youth"). This reality game show always began with the participants introducing themselves with an "I Am From" poem. This poetic format is inspired by a poem "Where I'm From" by George Ella Lyon. It follows a simple format that begins with "I am from" and continues with a fill-in-the-blank style of writing. For example, I am from–*describe home landscape*; I am from–*name three foods*; I am from–*name two problems you face every day.*

We chose this format because it delivered to the audience personal and relevant information in a short amount of time. It humanized our participants in a novel way by taking select strengths and vulnerabilities, and placing them in a structure, a poetic system. But the format felt safe because everyone was responding to the same prompt: the playing field was even. We learned that this format is a poetic and creative way for a person to present themselves to the world in a safe and playful way.

## In the Classroom

- Create your own "I Am From" Template. Aim for 10-12 lines and try to mix fun (music, sports, passions) with personal (heroes, family traditions). There are numerous iterations online to help you craft your template. Ask students to fill it out. The writing can be done individually in 10-30 minutes depending on the students' writing ability and grasp of the concept. You can write/share your own "I Am From" beforehand to both introduce the concept, as well as introduce yourself in a new light.
- You may want to request that each student add one or two new lines prior to the concluding line. These two additional lines become their own personal spin on the format, allowing them to cover ideas that are important to them. Those lines might include references to childhood toys or TV shows; games; religious beliefs; or favorite books.
- Have each student read their "I Am From" poem in front of the other students, keeping in mind that this format does require a level of vulnerability and students may want to limit their disclosures or opt out altogether. Needless to say, this should be respected.

## Digital Incentive

This format lends itself to multiple interpretations by expanding the format into video.

- The Single Reading: The simplest approach is to recite their poem directly to camera. Memorized or read. One shot, no edits. Having to perform one's "I Am From" poem changes the experience.
- The Paired Reading: Pair students together. After writing their own poems, partners then switch and read and record their partner's poem in the third person (i.e., "She is from . . ."). In this scenario, the pairs are introducing each other. Consider contrasting this with recordings of how they introduce themselves in the standard "I Am From" format. Consider how the voice and body language change when introducing someone else. Why is that?
- Group Reading or Montage: Working in groups of three, students record their own "I Am From" poems. Then students edit them together in a way that allows the differences or similarities in the answers to further elucidate the authors and who they are, through contrast and comparison. The experience here is that your understanding of the poets is now situated inside of a context: that of the other team members. It's like adding a frame to a picture: the new context brings out new meaning.
- Group Portrait: Use this format to explore the entire class or community. Each student writes their own poem. Working in groups, students then analyze each other's poems, looking for commonalities among the community. In the end, rewrite the poem as a class—expand the poem's format as desired—and record the poem as a "We Are From" piece. You can record this in any number of ways—in unison, taking turns, with choreography, through numerous edits . . . it's up to the students.

## Conclusion

This activity introduces original poetry writing to students through a personalized window. That personalization means that the students don't have to make things up or "create." By recording it, the students have to perform it—they have to explicitly consider approaches to presenting themselves. This is no longer a fleeting moment in the front of the classroom: it's being recorded. That media element allows the students to explore their public personas and work on their public-speaking skills, exploring basic techniques like speaking slowly, practicing memorization, looking at the camera, building in dramatic pauses, and thinking about the emotions embedded in particular lines. In the end, by digitally incentivizing this, one can compare the initial reading to the produced reading or group product and note the differences in understanding and content.

# Essay Analysis: Taking Control!

**Language Arts, History, STEAM:** nonfiction analysis; comparative media analysis; reading and vocabulary; author's perspective; human skills

**Digital Media:** video; audio voice-over; text graphics

**Time:** one to two weeks

## Introduction

In almost every state and national set of standards in the United States, "reading informational texts" (or some variation of this phrasing) is identified as one of the primary areas of focus for all students. As important as this task is—and it is positively critical to understanding the layers of thought that can only be articulated in writing forms such as essays, op-eds, and newspaper articles—it is a very difficult task to teach creatively and engagingly.

The task usually involves assigning an essay for the students to read; asking students to summarize the salient points or the central idea of the text; and then debating the intentions and meaning of that essay in class. You may spend time looking at the essay's title and determine its intentions. You may focus on specific word choices that convey this or that meaning. But there aren't a whole lot of creative strategies out there to help you teach how to read an essay.

Until now. . . . In this digital incentive, the main idea is to transfer ownership of the meaning of the essay from the author to the student.

## Digital Incentive

- Students work in pairs or groups of three. They are each assigned their own short essay with which to work. The ideal essay length for this activity is between 250 and 600 words. (The whole class can work on a single piece, but presenting their work is part of the final step, and it may not be productive to see or hear about the same essay over and over again.)
- Students work together to analyze the essay, identifying how the argument builds; the key words; and the general flow of the essay from start to finish. Their detailed analysis will allow them to move onto the next step.
- Each small group must re-present the essay, visually and aurally to the class, as a video. But the video can contain only the words themselves—text only. So, their tools are these: font choice and size, bolding, colors and pacing, placement on the screen (*Star Wars*, anyone?), text reveal, and so on. The

teams create a video of the text, to be seen and understood as the students *think* the essay should be seen and understood, as based on their prior analysis.

- Next, the students add an oral element. They record their reading of the essay, giving the inflection and emphasis where they think it is appropriate and speeding up, slowing down, and pausing as they deem necessary.
- You can request that the students add music and sound effects as well to offer one more aural tool to communicate their understanding of the essay and how to interpret it.
- There are numerous ways you can present this work. For example, present one essay traditionally: have students read the essay silently in class and then discuss. Contrast that with one group's digital presentation of their essay. Then discuss. What is the difference in the students' engagement with the content?

## Conclusion

The strength of this digital incentive is that the students have to take someone else's work, make it their own, and then sell it to the rest of the students. To do that successfully, they have to understand the mechanics of how the essay works effectively and then re-present those mechanics to the class, convincing them of the value of the original. They do this through brainstorming, collaborative analysis, and creative use of text on screen. They do this through speaking expressively and, perhaps, through the addition of music and sound effects. In the end, for each group of students, the work is not something external that they have to decipher but becomes something internal that they have to reproduce. And the other students—the audience—are given a new and dynamic way into complex and challenging content.

Please note that a link to student digital storytelling work that supports and complements the ideas and activities in this chapter can be found at www.meridianstories.com.

CHAPTER THREE

# Processing Learning

## Research, Creativity, Development, and Production

The website for the Common Core English Language Arts Standards opens with language that focuses on "critical thinking, problem-solving and analytical skills." They couch this language as a necessity–they use the word "required"–to succeed in life after secondary school (NGA Center and CCSSO 2021).

The introductory paragraph for the C3 Framework for Social Studies State Standards points to very similar skill sets, adding "participatory skills to become engaged citizens" (Silver Spring, MD: NCSS, 2013).

The nation's leading arbiter of science standards identifies the following skills as the most important in science education: communication, collaboration, inquiry, problem solving, and flexibility.

What is the common denominator among these leading organizations for learning standards? A focus on process. They all conclude their introductions with an emphasis on the process of learning, from critical thinking and participatory skills to problem solving and flexibility.

# Process Versus Outcome

There is a long-running debate in education about the tension between the values of outcomes versus processes. While I think it's fair to say that the majority of educators value process over outcome, formal education as an institution is driven more explicitly by outcomes. Therefore, we tend to teach to outcomes: the test scores.

I discovered a meaningful phrase in a remote corner of educational academia about this very issue:

> **A key part of education . . . is that it *seeks to develop new knowledge* (italics mine) rather than just mastering what is already known. It seeks creativity and originality. (Creasy 2018, 5)**

Such a majestic, powerful statement. Seeking new knowledge. I love the simplicity of that. Mastering content is a part of education. That is related to outcomes. Fine. Cool. We are all in. *But* "seek[ing] creativity and originality"—new knowledge—is about process. And while seeking new knowledge may be setting the bar high for middle or high schoolers, we do want to lay the foundations for them to do so. That's how humanity progresses.

Digital storytelling, as a learning strategy, is 75 percent about process. Digital storytelling is invested in the ideas articulated earlier in this book that assert what students need most of all to prepare for their futures are human skills—skills that will allow them to reach out and both touch and create knowledge. And those skills are bred inside of carefully scaffolded processes. It is one of the aims of this book to help shift the dynamics of the classroom toward a rebalancing of outcomes and processes. And one way to achieve that is through a project-based learning approach that has digital storytelling at its core.

It is an upstream journey. Assessment is often about mastery of knowledge, not about skill sets such as creativity and collaboration. Here's the crux of the dilemma: if you can cover a key World War II battle in one class, why spend three weeks on that battle with a digital storytelling project? The same question can be applied to any content to which you traditionally assign a single day.

And the answer is this: It's not about the battle. It's about learning and thinking and researching and problem-solving. It's about actively doing rather than absorbing. It's about creating your own story about history or literature, rather than accepting the story being told to you. The battle is, in essence, a means to a different learning end. It is not the end itself, despite what students are often led to believe. Emily Higgins, a middle and high school STEAM and special education teacher, puts it this way: "There is a tension between process and content. For me personally, I am a big process person, because with the process of learning and encouraging curiosity and creativity, which are things that I think about a lot, comes the content—it comes along with it in a more durable manner. And also lends itself to learning in the future. So, regardless of what you are learning, the process of integrating that information into your mind is what determines whether the information sticks around or not, in my mind."

Here's a slightly different pathway into this. Stanford professor of psychology Carol Dweck is renowned for her scientific research around the idea of a "growth mindset" versus the "fixed mindset." To understand a growth mindset is to talk about the power of "not yet" (Dweck 2014). As in, "I could either give you a D on this paper or I could grade you a 'not yet.'" The idea of not yet sees failure as an opportunity and not as a poor reflection of self. She argues that if students could see their struggles—and if teachers in turn reinforced those struggles—in the spirit of not yet, then the outcome for the student wouldn't be failure, but rather perseverance, resilience, deeper problem-solving capacities, iterative capacities, and, ultimately, self-confidence.

Dweck talks about an online math game that she developed with colleagues at the University of Washington:

> In this game, students were rewarded for effort, strategy, and progress. The usual math game rewards you for getting answers right, right now. But this game rewarded process. And we got more effort, more strategies, more engagement over longer periods of time, and more perseverance when they hit really, really hard problems. (2014)

Carol Dweck's approach is underpinned by both neurological science studies (more activity was measured in the brains of those who were trained in a growth mindset versus those who were not) and psychological science studies (students trained in "how they could learn to be smart—describing the brain as a muscle that became stronger the more it was used . . . showed marked improvement in grades and study habits" over a control group [Trei 2007]).

For our purposes, Dweck's work points to learning as, essentially, a matter of attitude, effort, and, ultimately, engagement. It makes the case that learning is essentially akin to a workout. Let's take a full moment inside of that analogy. Physical training is a workout of the body: a commitment to time and perseverance, a little pain usually. Learning is a workout of the brain: a commitment to time and perseverance, a little pain usually. In the end, you may be able to bench two hundred pounds or run a 5K in under thirty minutes. But those outcomes, like the battle from moments earlier, are just a means to an end—the stimuli for the workout in the first place. The real progress and growth; the development of the mental and physical resilience; the discipline to achieve: that's in the workout. The process.

And so it is in the classroom.

Figure 3–1

## Fancy Frogs—by Joe, Bucky, and Nova

Speaking of games and "not yet," take a moment to read this transcription of a video that three seventh graders made, documenting their process for creating a digital story about a board game designed to incorporate mathematics. The video style was pandemic-Zoom: three frames of their heads, talking, with one cutaway to the game board. As you read through this extraordinary discourse to nowhere—to no palpable outcome—consider the value of the journey they are sharing, the process they are documenting in all of its raw beauty. This is not your process exemplar. It's more your process actuality, for first-time digital storytellers.

**Joe:** Hi, my name is Joe.

**Bucky:** My name is Bucky.

**Nova:** And my name is Nova.

**Joe:** And this is our process of making our Meridian Stories project, Fancy Frogs. We started out looking through Meridian Stories and we picked some that we liked, but we decided to pick the board game one 'cause we thought that would be cool and have a lot of creativity in it. So we started out by thinking about different games that we liked and some of our favorite parts of those games, like in Life, we liked the board and in Catan, we liked the building parts, and we kind of started out from there, and we started to read the instructions, and just thinking on how we're going to do this.

**Bucky:** With the idea of the board games put together, we kind of realized that we needed a first draft, a rough draft of the board shape. So we made one and we knew this wouldn't be our final board [*picture of board*], but it was just something to go off. And as we were thinking of the board idea, we were thinking about the playing pieces and other functions of the game, so we thought that we could do building and that is how you reach the end. Like you could build the tallest tower, or a tower to a certain height, or you could, like, make a really long board and get to the end, and stuff like that. We never really finished deciding that, at that point in time.

**Joe:** We also then realized that we weren't thinking about the documentary at all. So we started thinking about different ways we could make the documentary. Like, we could film it like a commercial, selling it maybe. We could also have it, like, people playing the game. We also thought, like, how we could have the board game in it. Are we gonna just show pictures or are we going to actually play it in real time?

**Bucky:** We started back to thinking about the game instead of the documentary. And while we weren't really finished with our idea, we were out of time, so we brought it back to our advisory so we could have more opinions on the matter. We started thinking about playing pieces and at first we thought that they could be just random shapes like a triangle or a pyramid or something like that. But someone in our class brought up the idea that our playing pieces could be frogs. We didn't really know how we could pull it off—how we could make them—so we just set that aside and didn't really think much of it.

**Joe:** [*Interrupting*] Oh, yeah, we had lots of ideas but we weren't, umm, making decisions. We kept saying that we were going to, like, make a decision about the ending of the game, but we always just ended up making more ideas. But that's when Nova came along.

**Nova:** And I actually tried to make decisions.

**Joe:** So, after Nova came, we started making lots more decisions. We also got through the introduction, or the rules, and what we actually had to do to play the board game. And we saw that we needed math in it, so we started thinking that maybe we could have dice in it, as probability. We also started thinking that we could have a spinner as our mover, but we didn't think that that would be easy to pull off.

**Bucky:** So we came up with the idea of cards with questions on them and we thought, oh, the cards could have questions about your peers. But we realized that different people, if this ever did become a real game, would play it all around the world, or whatever, and so we realized that that wouldn't work very well, so we were thinking we could have the player write down stuff about their peers, but that wouldn't work either because not a lot of people would want to write just to play a fun game. So we came up with the idea of trivia.

**Joe:** So, after scrapping the witchcraft idea, we really didn't have a real theme for the game. So, maybe the frog part of the game could actually work. We started making questions about frogs and different levels of questions and . . .

**Bucky:** Depending on how hard the question was would depend on what type of token you got. So, for example, like, if you answered a really hard question, you could get a token that's worth, I don't know, twelve points, and you could buy a certain place with the coins so you could progress and have more of a chance. But it's also fair to your peers because even if you are going to get some dice that could go up to twelve, you could still get a one. It's fair to everyone and it's just fun.

# Process Disentangled

Education is chock-full of processes that are designed to optimize learning. The following three are in the fore of education at the time of this writing:

> **Inquiry-Based Science:** One source, an esteemed professor of education from Australia, Dr. Robyn Gillies, says, "Inquiry-based science adopts an investigative approach to teaching and learning where students are provided with opportunities to investigate a problem, search for possible solutions, make observations, ask questions, test out ideas, and think creatively and use their intuition" (2014).
>
> **Design Thinking:** According to the Teaching and Learning Lab (n.d.) at the Harvard Graduate School of Education, "Design Thinking is a mindset and approach to learning, collaboration, and problem-solving. In practice, the design process is a structured framework for identifying challenges, gathering information, generating potential solutions, refining ideas, and testing solutions."
>
> **Project-Based Learning (PBL):** PBLWorks (n.d.), a reputable organization that supports PBL exclusively, defines PBL as "a teaching method in which students gain knowledge and skills by working for an extended period of time to investigate and respond to an authentic, engaging, and complex question, problem, or challenge."

Digital storytelling is not a philosophy like these three examples. It doesn't ask you to approach everything you do through a singular framework. And it doesn't ask you to limit your content to solving real-world problems. No. Digital storytelling can work beautifully inside of these frameworks and even expand upon them by reaching beyond the "authentic learning" construct and including fantasy, originality and creativity, and problem-solving through art.

In digital storytelling, there is a clear process that can be applied across the board—a process that has deep resonances with the three approaches in the previous list but is framed more organically around storytelling. It follows an intuitive research, create, develop, and produce model.

## Research

The digital storytelling process begins with the content. You can't tell a story about something you know nothing about. So, you need to know the content. You research. And the research often organically invites primary sources. Why? Because the digital story construct favors humanizing the content and therefore often demands an intimate knowledge of the details of an event or a character's life.

You can't re-create Eleanor Roosevelt unless you encounter her own words. Perhaps words spoken in her home. So, where did she live and what was that house like? Hyde Park? Yowza! She lived there?! Why was she so rich? . . . And so it goes, down the exciting rabbit hole of primary sources. To tell a good story, you are going to want to know all you can about the content. The process begins with research.

Here is what Matt Loera, a seventh-grade history teacher, had to say about the digital storytelling projects in his classroom:

> **"The compelling part of the assignment is that the self-guided research conducted by the students *far* exceeds the level and complexity of the research they conduct on other assignments. With the challenge of telling a compelling story, the teams do exhaustive research, discuss their findings, and share information in exponential fashion."**

And here's the key in the classroom: don't let the student begin the creative development until they have convinced you of their mastery of the content. They will beg you to begin shooting. Don't let them. Push them and push them to dig further in this research phase. They will be rewarded with a much richer story to tell.

## Creativity

When I open a book—a serious work of fiction or nonfiction—I can't wait to read the first line. Sooo much dwells in the confines of that first line. Power. Language command. Story instigation. Voice. Control. Inspiration. It's like a thing with me: how will the author commandeer my attention and imagination in the first line?

So, there I was confronting the start of Edward Wilson's *The Origins of Creativity* (2017). I mean, who would even venture to take a stab at that question: the origins of creativity? The hubris! *But*, this is Edward Wilson, winner of two Pulitzer Prizes (that's insane) and a world-renowned scientist, naturalist, and writer. I bought the book without a second thought.

Then the moment. The opening sentence. And here it is:

> **Creativity is the unique and defining trait of our species; and its ultimate goal, self-understanding: What we are, how we came to be, and what destiny, if any, will determine our future historical trajectory. (3)**

Wow. But what does he really mean by that? He answers in the passage that immediately follows:

> **What, then, is creativity? It is the innate quest for originality. The driving force is humanity's instinctive love of novelty—the discovery of new entities and processes, the solving of old challenges and disclosure of new ones, the aesthetic surprise of unanticipated facts and theories, the pleasure of new faces, the thrill of new worlds. We judge creativity by the magnitude of the emotional response it evokes. (3)**

If this book in your hand could play a symphonic sting, I would insert it here.

In the creative step, students really are on "an innate quest for originality." They have never created a movie trailer before about a seminal US Supreme Court decision. They have never tried to tell a funny but serious story about cows, methane, and climate change. They have never produced a podcast about the critical relationship between local journalism and a healthy democracy. So, in that sense, this really is a quest for originality.

In the creative step, students make the decisions about story structure. The digital storytelling prompt should provide a lot of guidance here because the students need to be answering questions about characters, tone, story genre, use of graphics and online imagery, setting, casting, language choices, sound design, and visual design. The creative step—like all four steps in the digital storytelling process—doesn't have a clear start and finish: creativity is occurring throughout. But it does erupt here, after the research, when the team needs to decide how it is going to use text, sound, music, and imagery to tell a compelling story.

## Development

Development is what, in the media industry, is referred to as preproduction. This is about the logistics of planning the shoot or recording session. As just mentioned, students are still making creative choices throughout development. Costuming can shift. Locations can shift. Scripting is a fluid process. In fact, *the whole thing is a fluid process* and that is what makes it so compelling and rich educationally.

But the essence of development is in the planning and organization. A checklist of development may include the following:

- **Script:** Is the script finalized and does everyone who needs a script have one?
- **Rehearsals:** The team needs to schedule rehearsals. Perhaps they'll begin with a read-through and then move into the space in which they will be shooting.
- **Directing:** Who is directing, and are they making it up as they go along or planning their shots ahead of time?
- **Location Scouting:** Where are they going to shoot, and do they have or even need permission to shoot there?
- **Props:** Who is in charge of props? Who is taking charge of making sure that the whiffle ball bats for the fight scene are where they should be, when they should be?
- **Scheduling:** Often the biggest challenge is getting all the right people to the right place at the right time. With sports, music, drama, test prep, tutoring, ride availability, and so on, it can be hard to even figure out what that time is. Who's in charge of that?

Development is all about planning. It's about details. It's about logistics. If everyone agrees to shoot on Saturday morning in the playground, but no one checks the weather—monsoon coming!—then the shoot won't work. Planning. Details. Logistics.

I know. You see those three words and match them up to your students and conclude that this will be a massive challenge. And you are right: the development phase will feature failure . . . from which the students will rebound. It's an iterative process. They just keep going at it. For the students, the development phase is parenting, teaching, supervising, and socializing all in one. It's a little like playacting at being adults. And the assumption here is that that is a very good thing.

## Production

If development is planning, then production is executing. It's the shoot. The visual edit. The sound edit. It's the decision about which online images to use and what music will underscore this moment or that moment. It's the part where students must work together to bring their vision from the paper to the screen.

It's also about taking a deep dive into permissions and rights. Are their images and sounds royalty-free? What might work from the public domain? What is allowable for use under the Creative Commons Licensing structure or the Doctrine of Fair Use? That whole piece can get complicated. It's a learning curve—*for everyone*! My recommendation is to treat it as such; as an incremental learning process that will, over time, be ingrained into their work ethic.

This is not a production book designed to teach you about the ins and outs of production. As is indicated in the very first chapter, you don't need to know the ins and outs of media production. That is the students' literacy, not necessarily yours. There is a basic process that goes something like this:

- Create a shot list.
- Shoot the digital story.
- Record local ambient sound.
- Edit a rough cut of your story and share with trusted friends. Does it make sense? Are there some shots missing? Should the order of the shots be shifted?

  → If you are wondering what the best video or audio editing app for your students is, visit "EdTech Reviews and Resources" on the Common Sense Education website, a trusted destination for practical, quality media resources.

- Re-edit the rough cut, adding text and graphics as planned, and "lock picture"—no more visual editing.
- Apply your sound design plan, adding ambient sound, sound effects, and music.
- Double-check all your rights and permissions issues.

  → Meridian Stories has an online Digital Rules Center, which is designed to answer all the students' questions about rights and usage.

- Complete your sound edit and upload.

This process, honestly, will be pretty instinctive to your students. It's the natural order of how to put together a digital story. But take a look at those bullet points. Unpack that list for a moment, from your perspective. Look at the organization, communication, collaboration, digital literacy skill sets, creative vision, story curation, and time management issues that go into this phase. Just having to work through that process is a deeply educational experience unto itself.

**Research–Creativity–Development–Production**

Let's replace with synonyms:

**Investigating–Brainstorming–Planning–Doing**

Process *is* content.

---

**Figure 3–2**

In 2013, as Meridian Stories was just taking off, I conducted a survey of middle school students in three schools about the appeal and comprehension of learning through digital storytelling. I wanted to see if my hunches about this approach were correct. I surveyed 132 students. The word *challenge* in the statements on the survey refers to the digital storytelling assignment. All of these students had worked on one or two digital storytelling challenges before completing the survey.

I gave students the following list of statements with these directions: "Please rate each statement below using a ten-point agreement scale where 1 means you strongly disagree and 10 means you strongly agree."

All percentages are rounded up or down to the nearest whole number.

| The Statement | Percentage of Students Rating Statement Between 1 and 5 | Percentage of Students Rating Statement Between 6 and 10 | Most Popular Rating |
|---|---|---|---|
| This experience allowed me to work more independently from my teacher than I normally do. | 41% | 59% | 7 (20%) |
| My experience with the challenge was positive and rewarding. | 36% | 64% | 8 (17%) |
| I was able to handle the technological demands of the challenge with relative comfort. | 26% | 74% | 9 (20%) |
| Working on a team made this experience interesting, fun, and rewarding. | 27% | 73% | 10 (23%) |
| I feel like I learned more about the topic through working on the challenge than if the topic had been taught in a more traditional style. | 31% | 69% | 10 (21%) |
| Working on this challenge has made me more interested in the topic. | 47% | 53% | 5 (21%) |
| Creating media for school projects feels like it adds significant value to my schooling experience. | 38% | 62% | 7 and 8 (tied at 15%) |

*(continues)*

*(continued)*

My takeaways from this informal survey of students include the following:

- Consistently, the students rated the learning experience more favorably rather than less favorably. In fact, way more favorably. It's not even close. And that's the *headline*.
- Statement 4, about collaboration, received the most top ratings of 10, suggesting that despite the many fears about and difficulties with collaborating effectively, working with one's peers definitively increased their engagement with the experience.
- Statements 5 and 7 showed highly significant differences in the percentages between the lower and higher ratings. And they both used the phrase *feels like*, as in "I feel like I learned more" and "feels like it adds significant value." This points to the educational experience itself as a positive one, as one that perhaps reinforced their self-confidence and altered their attitude about time in school. Perception matters.
- Statement 6, while being the one that revealed more or less a balance between disagreement and agreement, nevertheless stands out as a positive. How often is it that a project engenders *more* interest in that topic? Hopefully you can snag a handful of students with each area of focus, but that the *majority* stated an increased interest is, I would hazard to guess, a victory.

---

# Spirited Activities for the Classroom

What follows are ideas and activities that are designed to creatively explore and interrogate essential components of the digital storytelling process, past the initial research phase:

- creative brainstorming (creativity)
- character building (creativity)
- setting and visual design (creativity and development)
- creating storyboards (development)
- framing the shot (production)

# Creative Brainstorming

More than half the fun of writing and producing a story is brainstorming that story. At the very start, students find themselves on the edge of creative possibility: they are about to create a world of characters and events that is new and original. What follows are some fun, gamelike approaches to brainstorming to help your students get the idea going. Pick one or more, then go. And as you are doing this, keep in mind these words from Edward Wilson:

> We judge creativity by the magnitude of the emotional response it evokes. (2017, 3)

ACTIVITY

## Brainwriting

The term *brainwriting* and general methodology were formalized by a German author, Bernd Rohrbach, in 1968 (Wikipedia 2020).

- The approach begins with a creative problem to solve. It can be specific or general. For example:
  - When the characters enter the transport machine, where are they sent and why?
  - The topic is bullying. It's the first day of summer camp. What does Joshua do that is so embarrassing he wants to go back home that night?
  - The story is about the main ideas that informed the establishment of the League of Nations in 1920. What's the hook?
  - What's the one experience in Ella's backstory that has shaped her the most?
- In groups of three to six, each student gets one piece of paper. Everyone has three minutes to write down three ideas in response to the problem to be solved. These ideas should be unedited—whatever comes to mind.
- After three minutes, everyone passes their paper to the group member on their left. Everyone reads the ideas previously written to themselves and has another three minutes to write down three more ideas. They can use the ideas already written as inspiration for new ones, or they can ignore them altogether.
- Repeat this process until everyone has their original sheet back. Then, as a group, share answers, choose the five best, and present these creative solutions to the rest of the class—who may be working on the same creative problem or a different one.

This activity is adapted from "Brainwriting," by the Mind Tools Content Team (n.d.).

ACTIVITY

## Random Idea Starters

This strategy can be a good way to spark the initial idea that will become the story: a new work of collaborative fiction. This can be done in small groups or as a whole class.

- Have each person pick two random stimuli—a word, a number, an image, a song title, or an object from the dictionary, the internet, or the TV—and write each idea on a scrap of paper.
- Students fold their papers, place them in a hat or container, and then pull one out at random.
- Students have a brief discussion about story ideas that might incorporate whatever is written on the paper. (Example: A cuckoo clock on the wall could inspire them to create a story that takes place inside the clock's machinery where the cuckoo bird lives.)
- Students repeat until they have considered all the papers. Or, midway through, they can pick two pieces of paper from the hat and create a story around both of those words.

ACTIVITY

## What If?

This is a tool more than a straight-up activity. But it's a powerful tool, because those two words *what if*—just those words—are designed to spark speculation and the imaginative spirit. Think about the moment when someone turns to you with a spark in their eye and says, "What if . . . ?" A world of possibility flashes in front of you at that moment. The possibility of a solution hangs in the air. Here are some places to apply this linguistic lever in the classroom.

### To Open Up Curricular Content

*What if* is a phrase that asks students to defy physics, science, and history as they know it. It's a classroom conversation starter, a back-alley way into challenging topics. For example:

- What if the moon got knocked off its orbital course by a powerful meteor?
- What if there was no more market for Saudi oil—what would happen to the wealth of Saudi Arabia?
- What if the songbird population doubled? Would there be a noise problem?

In these cases, the what-if question provides an unexpected, creative pathway into content exploration about ecology, physics, global history, and so on. It's like a secret passageway into tough questions. The popular Amazon Prime series *Man in the High Castle* is solely premised on a what-if question: What if the Germans and Japanese had won World War II? Another popular series, *Black Mirror*, is almost solely based on asking what-if questions of our technologies and playing out the consequences.

### To Solve Creative Dilemmas

The process of story creation constantly runs into dead ends. The characters don't appear to have any way out of a situation. Or the characters aren't making interesting decisions. Or your students land on very implausible solutions that, in the end, sink the story. Story creation is hard. Really hard. Bring on the what-if questions to get them—your students and their characters—out of sticky situations or bring life to an otherwise lifeless tale. For example:

- What if there is a blackout right at that moment?
- What if he is, in fact, her son, and he doesn't know it?
- What if, as she is storming out of the room, the door gets stuck? Or the elevator gets stuck?
- What if there's a knock at the door? Or your character gets a text message from her mom . . . right at that moment?!
- What if he's highly allergic to those eggs he's eating? Or the cat he's snuggling with? What then?

"What if . . . ?" is a question that allows you and the students to change the trajectory of a story in an instant. If it's a group creative problem, have everyone in the group write down two what-if questions and then share.

### To Start a Story

If the activity at hand is to write or produce a creative story, the what-if? tool is one way to get the creativity going. Take something known, undo it, and then play with the consequences. For example:

- What if certain trees grew clothing instead of fruit? There would be sock trees and sweater trees . . . .
- What if books were still scrolls or the alphabet had two hundred letters instead of twenty-six?
- What if the internet were available for only one hour a day?

# Building Characters

In my view, character is the most important creative element in a story. Emotional identification and resonance happen through character. Looked at another way and speaking very broadly, our personal happiness is often premised on our friends and families. The real characters in our lives. And so too with the fictional characters in our lives. Not the plots. Or the settings. The characters. I think it's fair to say that we all love Hogwarts, but it's the characters—Harry, Hermione, Hagrid, Dumbledore, McGonagall, Dobby—that bring that world to life.

To create a fictional character, your students will need to know (1) the character's backstory and (2) their future story.

## Backstory

When you arrive in a room, you arrive with a full physical presence on the outside and an entire history of decisions, actions, experiences, likes, and dislikes on the inside. As writers, your students need to know their character's outside and inside like they know themselves. To achieve this, begin with what you already know.

## Create Your Character Based on People You Know

There is no reason for your students to invent a new character (that is very hard work and it's even harder to make that person believable!) when they are inevitably surrounded by so many interesting characters already. Ask them to look around, and as they do so, ask these questions: "Who fascinates you? Whom do you know on their inside? What are the dominant traits of four of the most interesting people around you?" Then direct them to use that information to create a new character. For example, take the picky food-eating habits of one friend; the spacey, flighty language patterns of another; the piercing, see-through-to-your-soul stare of another; and the love of the saxophone of a fourth friend, mix them all together, and . . . you have the start of a really interesting character: a fifteen-year-old girl who talks as if she is adrift, has small obsessions like her food choices, can zero in on someone in an unusually focused way when she hears a certain tone of voice that she finds offensive, and lets loose with her saxophone, producing music that is exactly like how she thinks.

ACTIVITY

## Known Person Descriptors

Students work in groups. Each student picks someone they know—preferably someone that the other group members won't know—and writes a one-page description of that person, freestyle, as if they were describing this person to their family or best friend. Have your students read their write-ups aloud to their group, debate the descriptions, and discuss how this group of new characters meets the needs of the project and how they would or would not get along with each other.

ACTIVITY

## Questioning Character

The next step is to ask questions of their character so that students can begin to fill this person out. These include questions relating to the character's economic class; dress habits; likes and dislikes; top skills; biggest fears; and outlook, whether it be optimistic or pessimistic.

Each individual group member comes up with ten questions for their character. They can think of questions that they would want to ask a celebrity, for example, or someone on whom they have a deep crush. They share the questions and answer them, filling out the dimensions of their new character.

In the end, their goal is to know that character on the outside and the inside. The goal is *not* to make a list of character traits. A list is just a list, not a representation of a character. A character is someone whom you know nearly like yourself.

### Future Story

This part is very, very straightforward. In order to create a character's future story, the students need to constantly put them in a situation that requires them to make a decision.

*A character is based on the decisions they make.*

Will he lie or not? Will she study or not? Will they hate or forgive? Will she try harder or give up? Will he cry or keep it all in? Will they yell and scream or whisper? Will he dress up or dress down? Will they tell the truth or cover up?

ACTIVITY

## Location Scout

In the movie business there is a person called a location scout. This is the person who is in charge of finding all the right locations for a movie. They may get an assignment that reads something like, "Scene takes place in mossy, wet gorge that feels unvisited by humankind." The location scout has to find that place.

Have your students scout a location connected to a literary, scientific, or historical story you are studying. Let's imagine Richard Wright (1908–1960), author of *Black Boy* and *Native Son* (among many other publications), were coming to your neighborhood to be interviewed. Have them research Richard Wright. What in the background of his life in Mississippi, Chicago, and Paris, France, would help shape their choice of a place to speak with him? Think in terms of setting as character: *whom* would your students want him to be with, from your town or neighborhood? This is not an easy question or activity. It's abstract. Ask the students to take three photos from their location search. Off the students go, actively looking for the nooks and crannies in the neighborhood that will (1) be visually interesting and (2) enhance the narrative.

This activity serves three purposes. First, it provides a unique pathway into researching a figure whom you are studying. Second, it contextualizes your studies inside of your community: how do history, language arts, or STEAM and your community connect in this regard? And third, it brings to the fore the importance of setting in your students' gradual mastery of digital storytelling.

ACTIVITY

## Visual Style Guide

In the movies, there is also a visual designer, whose job it is to create a cohesive visual style for the movie, which usually translates to a defined color palette and a visual tone, spirit, and texture. Think urban chic: sleek, beiges and grays, shiny, minimalist. Or think distressed ruin: decrepit, dusty corners, faded hues of red and blue, poorly lit, wood everywhere.

Have your students create what's called a visual style guide for their digital story—just one page. Or they can do this for a short story that they are reading or a historical scene that they are studying. The visual style guide is designed to suggest the setting and overall look of a scene to be shot around your assigned content. It should contain (1) a defined color palette and (2) three to four images—either original or pulled from the internet—that communicate the look, tone, and texture students are going for, for this character known as *setting*.

In all of these cases, the idea is to get students thinking actively about the role of setting and location in their digital stories. The more sensitive they are to the entire visual spectrum of their storytelling, the better their stories will be. And while these activities may appear to be a little off the main line of curricular content, they will force the students to look at that content in new ways, which will empower them to actually design the curricular experience for the viewer. That's powerful.

# Creating Storyboards

A storyboard is a series of panels of rough sketches—simple drawings—outlining the sequence of scenes or major changes of action in a digital story.

Here's another way to look at it: You know when you ask your students to write an outline of their ideas before they begin to write the paper? A storyboard is the same thing, except pictures replace the words. A storyboard is a visual outline of the key camera shots or scenes, in their correct order, which serves as the framework for recording (or animating) their story.

A storyboard should convey some of the following information:

- which characters are in the frame and how they are moving;
- what the characters are saying, if anything;
- how much time has passed between the storyboard frames; and
- what kind of camera shot is being featured.

The visual information is inside the panels. The written information—either describing the action or directly quoting key dialogue—is under each panel.

In general, there aren't hard-and-fast rules to storyboarding, so there are no definitive rights and wrongs. It is a tool to help the students plan their media experience. An internet search of "storyboard samples" will reveal a host of examples that should guide you to a model that best suits the needs of your classroom.

## Outlines Are a Drag; Storyboards Are Fun

Here's the thing: storyboarding is a tremendous value-added, academic activity. It's about organization, collaboration, visual thinking, planning, problem-solving, and storytelling. But storyboarding *can* be perceived as this interim step that you are insisting upon just to make their lives a tad more miserable. In short, it can be perceived to be as much of a drag as that traditional paper outline.

But it doesn't have to be this way. Storyboards are essentially comic books. They are messy and fun—drawings that can go outside of the lines. They are pictorial. They are windows into one's story that one wouldn't have seen otherwise. Consider letting the students own the format as much as possible. That may open up new possibilities.

Let's begin with a storyboard activity that is simultaneously easy and complex, labor intensive but not laborious. One that will allow students with different skill sets—the artist, the researcher and fact gatherer, the storyteller, the script writer—to work together to be a part of the process.

ACTIVITY

## Four-Frame Storyboarding

Try beginning with a four-frame storyboard that is designed to indicate a sixty-second digital story. One piece of paper split into quadrants. This four-frame storyboard can be about any topic that you are studying. Imagine a four-frame storyboard about . . . a Latin American city; the science of the tides; the climax of a book; deforestation and its consequences. Under each frame, the students are allowed ten words maximum. The words can be descriptive or, more poignantly, scripted words: what the characters or voice-over would be saying. This four-frame storyboard is about finding two things:

1. The four most important images that will communicate the essence of their story; and
2. The movement of the story through these images—in other words, how one image leads the way to the next and on through to a triumphant ending.

The students may have, in their minds, many other images and words in between. That's fine: a sixty-second story could have anywhere from thirty to sixty edits. This is about the four highlights; the narrative pinnacles; the critical content points of your students' story. This is asking them essentially: What are the most potent images and how are they communicating with each other?

Finally, the storyboard is a perfect marker for you to understand your students' work before they begin shooting. The script is one way into checking their progress. But the storyboard reveals many more layers.

I have had success in teacher training workshops with this particular four-frame storyboarding challenge, called Global Team Building:

> **Since its inception, the United Nations Security Council has had five permanent member countries: China, France, Russia, the United Kingdom, and the United States. With their veto authority, each of these permanent members carries enormous power over UN deliberations.**
>
> **The world has changed significantly since the end of World War II when the UN was formed and the victors granted themselves permanent seats and veto authority. Now, more than seventy years later, the map of global economic and political power looks very different. The Security Council no longer represents the modern geopolitical reality, and many argue that it is therefore hampering real progress in the UN's deliberations.**
>
> **Your challenge is to propose a new and improved UN Security Council, by suggesting one more country you think should be added to the current group of five. Then, storyboard and script a sixty-second video and, *using no more than four shots*, build your case for adding just one of these countries. This challenge is only sixty seconds. This suggests that the focus of this is on your verbal argument and your speaker. *But* your medium is visual. So, be sure to also ask these questions: With just a maximum of four shots, how can we make the most visual impact? How can we visually reinforce and enhance our verbal positions within these limitations?**

Some of the resulting storyboards are shown in Figure 3–3.

Figure 3–3

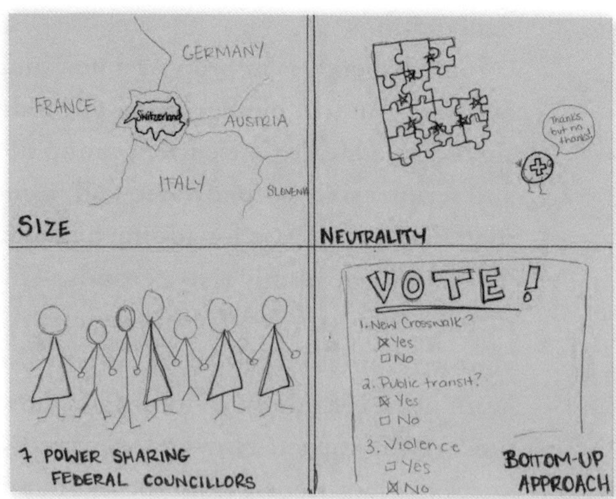


## The Shot List

The primary purpose of these two storyboarding activites is to continue to push students to think about how images communicate, especially in contrast to words. However, these activities open the door to a very practical application: the planning of a shot list. The more traditional storyboard—say, a twelve- or twenty-four-frame storyboard—is a step that (1) helps to visualize and concretize the story in a detailed fashion and (2) impels the creation of a shot list. A filmmaker's storyboard is a sequencing of shots in the order in which the story is going to be told. A shot list is a list of shots in the order in which they will be shot. The former is for creative purposes (anticipating and planning for the visual narrative) and the latter is for practical purposes (knowing how many shots for each location, for each actor, at what time of day). So, while the story may open and close on a park bench, the shot list tells us that we need five shots on the park bench. The student team will shoot those shots in one time period, rather than shooting in chronological (or storyboard) order, going back and forth and all over the place. The shot list: it's an incredibly useful step that saves so much time and confusion down the line. Think organization, time management, planning, problem-solving. And from whence does it come? The storyboard.



# Framing the Shot

Planning your digital story or creating a storyboard often demands that you make decisions about camera shots. There are a variety of different kinds of shots from which to choose when putting together your visual vision.

The best way for students to increase their awareness about camera shots is to watch some movies or TV series. These narrative forms, as opposed to YouTube or most of the social media platforms, generally employ professionally trained directors who have very explicitly selected each shot—and sequence of shots—in order to maximize the impact of their stories. In short, they choose camera angles very deliberately, from a depth of expertise, which makes them good models for teaching this sector of digital storytelling.

There are three kinds of shots that form the foundation of digital storytelling: the long shot, the medium shot, and the close-up.

## The Long Shot

The long shot is a wide shot and shows the location and the characters (if there are any). Many scenes open with a long shot or establishing shot, which establishes for the audience where the scene is taking place.

- **Football (American):** Every single play that is broadcast on TV begins with a wide shot. The audience needs to see the whole field and the positioning of all the players on both teams in order to anticipate how the play might unfold.
- **Sitcoms:** Many sitcoms begin with a wide or establishing shot of the exterior of the building in which the sitcom takes place. It might be the school or the home. This tells the viewer where we are; it establishes location.

## The Medium Shot

The medium shot is significantly closer to the action and shows more of the character and less of the location. A two-shot, in which two characters are talking to each other, is an example that is usually shot in a medium shot.

- **Football:** Once the play is unfolding—a run or a pass—there is usually a cut to a medium shot. This focuses the viewer on the action—not the whole field, but the important action of the moment. And it lets the viewer get closer to that action.
- **Sitcoms:** When sitcoms cut to the interior (inside the kitchen, the office, the school hallway), the shot is designed to frame the important characters. If there are two characters, then this requires a medium shot—a shot that focuses the viewer on the important characters in that scene but also indicates their general location. Sometimes if there are many characters, the shot will begin wide and then zoom into a medium shot.

## The Close-Up

The close-up shot is designed to show the facial expressions of the characters and is used during scenes with important dialogue or high emotion. The over-the-shoulder-shot, in which you are looking at one character talking from the perspective of the listener, is an example that is usually shot in close-up.

- **Football:** At the end of the play, there is usually a close-up. Now the camera can focus on the pileup of players or can attempt to show the smile or grimace of the players getting up from the tackle. The close-ups make the players human and emotional, revealing character in ways that the wide and medium shots can't.
- **Sitcoms:** Like the example with football, the close-ups are used to reveal character, to show funny facial reactions, sadness, silliness, disbelief, and so on. Seeing close-ups on the characters in turning-point moments is very rewarding for the viewers.

## Other Options

While those three types of shots cover 80 percent of what you'll see, there are numerous other angles and ways to frame a shot. When screening TV programs, have the students look for other types of camera shots that they can include in their inventory of choices for their digital story.

Here are two to consider incorporating:

- The high camera angle, which is shot from above and tends to make the subjects look small or weak.
- The panning shot, where the camera slowly moves across a scene (a landscape, an apartment room, a dinner table, etc.) from left to right or vice versa. They could use this type of shot to establish place, natural beauty, or decrepitude; create mystery and suspense (What are we looking for in this slow pan of the block?); or tell a very broad story of a place (a bustling city, a vibrant main street, or a stark contrast: a pan that begins on well-trimmed suburban lawns and ends on some overgrown, empty lots).

ACTIVITY

### Shots Shouted Aloud

Prepare to show three five-minute clips of any TV program in your classroom. With each cut or edit, shout out the kind of shot as it goes along: "Wide shot . . . close-up . . . close-up . . . over-the-shoulder close-up . . . medium two-shot . . ." You can start this activity and then have the kids pick it up, going around the room. Or just leave the whole thing open to your kids shouting the answers. Then after the five-minute segment, lead a brief discussion about how the sequence of shots helped to present a coherent story.

Consider watching a variety of formats, like a commercial, a sports program, a sitcom, and a TV drama. They all have distinct stories to tell, so they all present their shot sequences a little differently and at dissimilar paces. The more your kids study their favorite TV shows from this perspective, the better able they will be to storyboard and direct their own digital stories.

## Digital Storytelling Projects

What follows are three classroom activities from the Digital Incentive Series. They are designed to offer up an engaging approach to learning. These can be applied to history, English language arts, or STEAM classes—and by adding a digital layer, they make the learning and student engagement exponentially more powerful. In particular, these digital layers focus on the processes that digital storytelling comprises—research, creativity, development, and production—with a special emphasis on some of the select components in this chapter including characters, setting, and storyboarding. Each of these activities can take one or two classes, or one or two weeks, depending on how many of the digital options you want to pursue.

PROJECT

# Storyboarding Literary Characters

**Language Arts:** storyboarding; character analysis; literary analysis; human skills
**Digital Media:** photography; montage editing
**Time:** one to two weeks

## Introduction

For many students, writing is one of the most difficult ways to express themselves. It is, ironically, a wall to expression. And yet upon reading a short story or work of literature, these same students have many things to say about the characters and their motivations; the use of language by the author; and the sense of place or foreboding that the author has created. But writing that out may not be the best course of action.

In this digital incentive, we turn to storyboarding as a unique and expressive way for students—both writers and nonwriters—to communicate their understanding of literary texts.

## In the Classroom

- Give student pairs a sheet of poster board with three square panels drawn on it, plus markers and colored pencils (more or less: whatever you have!). In each of the three panels, they should illustrate a key moment in the life of one of the key characters from a novel or short story that you are reading. Or the assignment can be more specific, like three key moments in a chapter; it is up to you. The end objective is to communicate, in just three panels, an understanding of that character and their journey in the novel, short story, poem, play, or chapter.
- The pairs have one or two classes to debate among themselves which three moments are the most important moments and then to illustrate those moments. By working on a team, each member is exposed to the other's views on that character, leading to a deeper understanding through debate and decision-making.
- Ask students to pay particular attention to perspective. Is this storyboard frame drawn from a third-person or first-person point of view? Which point of view would best represent the team's portrayal of this character?

- Request that each panel contain at least three props, set pieces, or environmental indicators that will help inform the viewer's understanding of the character and their circumstances.
- You should explain that this is not a contest to see who has the best drawing skills; in fact, those who stress the drawing too much will not finish in time. Stick figures are fine. What's important here is that the storytellers have a clear idea for how to visually communicate the three moments they want to capture.
- Under each panel, the pairs can write one sentence using ten words or less. This condition can, of course, vary, depending on you and your students. The choice of ten words is designed to keep the focus on the illustrations and to stay within the storyboard format, using words to caption the illustrations rather than describe them. However, expanding this limit to include quotes directly from the reading—for example, one quote per panel, up to twenty-five words—could be more effective.
- There are a variety of ways to share these panels with the whole class. You can hang them around the room and let the class view them gallery-style, or each pair can present their storyboard to the class.

## Digital Incentive

- The digital incentive borrows from the notion of crowdsourcing. At this point you have, say, up to ten portraits of one, two, or three main characters at perhaps different stages within the novel. Now, put them together.
- Begin by having each group take photos of their work (one panel per photograph), which transforms their work into a digital storyboard.
- Working with all the content available, groups can now create a ten-frame storyboard of one character's full arc, reflecting an in-depth portrait. The new storyboard will represent different artistic styles; focus on a wide range of emotions and events; and allow for the convergence of different but complementary perspectives. In short, the new storyboard has transformed into a complex visual assessment of the novel's lead character or characters, representing different points of view in the class—in one visual experience.
- If desired, the students can add preprogrammed movement to this storyboard, as well as a soundtrack. In short, students can leave it as a simple sequence of frames, or "produce" it with as many audio bells and whistles as they want.

## Conclusion

This nontraditional approach, first and foremost, taps into visual intelligence—communicating (and understanding) through images, not words. As we all know, visual communication can be both limiting and transformative. This is a useful exercise for those who are not strong with writing *and* those who are. But a storyboard approach—as opposed to, say, a short essay—makes a new form of collaborative work possible. *That* is what makes this digital incentive unique and compelling. It's hard for two or three people to write an essay together. But it's not hard to merge different storyboards to form a more complete, nuanced portrait of a character.

PROJECT

# Facebook Profiles

**History and Language Arts:** biographical creation (historical figures, authors, fictional characters, etc.); social media; writing; human skills

**Digital Media:** social media page; text and graphics

**Time:** one to two weeks

## Introduction

This activity works for both language arts and history. The example here draws on history as our working sample.

A biography is a useful tool to understand an important figure's life. Using the words of the subject, interviews from people who knew the subject, and even other biographies, a biographer is able to decide how the world will see someone. In this activity, you will ask students to combine this traditional work with a new element: Facebook. Facebook can be seen as a personal snapshot of a moment—a week or day or month in their life, depending on usage. While a Facebook page has one's background information posted, it's more about what is happening to that person now. And this is a unique opportunity for students to humanize the historical figures that they are studying.

## In the Classroom

- Direct students toward a selection of historical figures that work with your curricular objectives.

- Working in pairs, students will use primary and secondary sources to research their figure. Information to consider includes:
  - → significant events that shaped the person's life
  - → significant societal events that this person influenced
  - → significant relationships, personal and professional
  - → significant places in the person's life—homes, places visited, etc.
  - → significant pleasures, pastimes, and preferences of this person
- Working inside of the Facebook structure, students lay out the information on a poster board in sections that include the headings "About," "Friends," and "Photos," and, most importantly, three sample posts. The posts can be from a range of time periods, indicating a few key moments in that figure's life.

## Digital Incentive

- The goal now is to pick a specific time in this person's life—a life-defining moment, perhaps—and construct four posts from this figure during the span of a week or month. What are they posting? Who is responding? How many likes? The idea here is to get inside the head of this figure and ask: What exactly does this person want to communicate to the world at this moment in time? What is the voice of this person on Facebook? If they are not famous (at this moment that has been chosen), are these posts mostly personal, or are they aware of their following and talking to a broader audience?
- Allow the students to choose their imagery from sources that are of the time or contemporary. This will give them the freedom to interpret the voice and perspective of their character broadly and with agency.
- Each post should include either a picture, a video, an infographic, or a meme; some text (as desired); and comments and likes.
- The platform for presenting these posts is up to the students. Pinterest can be a great source for gathering relevant images. Perhaps talk to your school IT person to recommend the most appropriate platform for presenting and organizing your students' four FB posts.

## Conclusion

Today, through social media, people are writing their own evolving autobiographies. They are telling stories about themselves, deciding what they want the world to see. In this activity, we ask the student to step into the shoes of a historical figure and broadcast what they see and feel. This requires the student to go beyond the historical facts that typically define our understanding of significant figures and research a way to humanize them: to understand them less as stock figures of history and more as one understands an uncle or an aunt. To try to capture their voice. Facebook is a stock and standard platform with which everyone is familiar. And so we turn to Facebook to help students capture that angle on these figures. And we focus on a singular time in their lives—something manageable—to bring students closer to these distant, historical figures.

### Language Arts Application

This works well for characters in a novel, short story, or play; imagine doing this with Fabiola from *American Street* (Ibi Zoboi), Pecola Breedlove from *The Bluest Eye* (Toni Morrison), Charlie from *The Perks of Being a Wallflower* (Stephen Chbosky), or Nick from *The Great Gatsby* (F. Scott Fitzgerald). For literary characters, students will need to find more abstract images than photos. Students could draw representations of the character, dress up as the character, or find images online. It also works for authors who share a literary heritage in terms of when they wrote, what they wrote about, or how they wrote.

---

PROJECT

## Forecasting History

**History and Language Arts:** current events analysis; historical research; presentational skills; understanding metaphor; human skills

**Digital Media:** graphic creation (still or moving); video shooting; media format exploration

**Time:** one to three weeks

### Introduction

This digital incentive looks at the inverse of history by looking *forward* in time and not backward. But of course, in order to successfully anticipate what *may* happen, we have to be informed by what has already happened: in short, history. So, this is about putting the students' knowledge of history to work in order to help us all understand what lies in front of us. And this is also about doing it playfully—inside of a weather-forecasting format.

The Weather Channel is dedicated entirely to forecasting the weather. A handful of other channels are dedicated to forecasting the political future of people and places. They are, among others, Fox News, CNN, MSNBC, and PBS.

In this activity we will take advantage of these synergies and ask students to become political scientist forecasters. Specifically, teams of students will produce a weather forecast about NATO or US-Mexico relations or coal production or climate change or Venezuela or Nigeria or China or Saudi Arabia. The topic is up to you. For the purposes of sampling, let's take Saudi Arabia.

Imagine a celebrity anchor from CNN in front of a map of Saudi Arabia, acting and sounding like a weather person but talking about oil, wealth, solar, and religion. What would she be saying and how is she using that map of Saudi Arabia behind her?

Using weather as your metaphor, students present a forecast for Saudi Arabia, looking ahead up to five years. Is there much-needed rain in the forecast? What is happening to the sandstorm that is spreading toward Qatar to the east and Egypt to the west? Will temperatures become too hot for those considering traveling there in the near future? Or will those temperatures simmer? Will Saudi political weather affect the political weather in the United States?

## In the Classroom

- Have students break into small groups. Either assign the topics or let them pick their own.
- Using primary and secondary sources, students research and identify at least three critical strategic objectives about their topic and corresponding obstacles their selected topic faces in achieving these objectives.
- You can define this also by having the students look at the topic through three different categories, such as economics, external relations with allies, and internal political stability. The idea is that limiting this to three inquiries keeps this manageable.
- In a playful way, students translate and reinterpret those political objectives and obstacles into a weather forecast, outlining the various possibilities that could occur depending on whether or not (for example) "the cold front hits like a polar vortex," "the storm makes land," or "the drought continues."
- Other important guidelines to consider:
    - → Teams can forecast into the future anywhere from six months to five years.
    - → Weather forecasting is more storytelling than it is news reporting. Correlatively, weather forecasters are more characters than they are news anchors or reporters. Of all the news formats, this one is the most playful and narrative-driven.

- → Weather forecasting is also about helping the audience prepare for the future: you watch the weather to help plan ahead. It's the same here: what are the students preparing their audience to understand and possibly prepare for?

- Have teams present their political weather forecasts.

## Digital Incentive

- Weather forecasts often involve two things on top of the written script: graphic visual displays and field correspondents who are on the scene where the weather is happening.
- Prompt your students to create up to three visual displays to accompany their forecast. These can be static graphics or moving graphics.
- Prompt your students to shoot one reporter on the scene. They could shoot that person in front of a green screen or on location, depending on their topic.
    - → Be sure to direct your students to spend some time watching weather forecasts on TV and listening to them on radio. It's useful if they identify two or three presentational elements they'll want to replicate in their presentation.

## Conclusion

This digital incentive asks students to put their knowledge of history to work to help prepare for the future. And it asks them to do it in a playful way. That delivers academic relevance and student engagement.

When you take this into the digital realm, the exploration of history leaves the page and becomes more tangible. By requiring graphics, you shift the weather-forecast format from a fun exercise to a presentation that requires research, rehearsal, and digital fluency. And by adding a field correspondent, you ensure that the students must try to understand their topic viscerally: what does this place or topic look and feel like, and how are they going to represent that?

Finally, this digital incentive asks students to understand and apply their knowledge of metaphors and how they work. These weather forecasts are metaphors for what is really happening in a country or around a topic. This allows them to play with language, words, and double entendre in ways that are rarely exercised in the classroom.

## Language Arts Applications

In addition to the creative writing inherent in this format, the forecasting piece could be applied to:

- characters, after students have completed reading a novel.
- proposed book sequels: what would happen in the next installment?
- the state of writing (or handwriting; published, hardcover books; or face-to-face conversations and debating) in a digital world.

Please note that a link to student digital storytelling work that supports and complements the ideas and activities in this chapter can be found at www.meridianstories.com.

CHAPTER FOUR

# The Curricular Ecstasies of Stories and Story Creation

When corporate executives and nonprofit leaders go on a retreat to sharpen their skills, one of the most popular areas of focus is storytelling. Professionals teach them how to tell stories. Why? Because good stories—about your nonprofit; about the kids whom you have benefited; about how your product has changed lives—engage and help secure donations or investments. Many would argue that out in the real world, command of storytelling is one of the most valuable skill sets to possess.

And yet storytelling as a formal form of humanities teaching, beyond elementary school, often isn't explicitly acknowledged or regularly practiced across the curriculum, a situation that has been eloquently challenged by Tom Newkirk in his book *Minds Made for Stories.*

I agree with Tom. This needs to change. Storytelling is humanity's most universal form of communication, from oral cultures to literate cultures, transcending all languages: the story, the tale, is a clear fundament of communication. If your students can tell a story about a literary character; the origins of a word; the process of photosynthesis; the motivations of a political leader; a day in the life of an ant; or the experiences of immigrants in your community, then there is a deep understanding of that topic. Why? Stories reveal deep understanding because the format of storytelling implicitly insists that you have a personal connection to the topic. You *know* this as a teacher: the best teachers are often the best because they are good storytellers. You can't tell an effective and engaging story unless that content is sitting comfortably in your head and under your skin—unless you've explored the hidden corners of the person or event or phenomenon. Stories aren't summaries, outlines, or book reports. They are communications that come from inside the storyteller. *That's the secret of this form of communication and its power: one's personal investment in and connection to the content.*

Here's another angle into the power of storytelling. I want to replace the phrase *personal investment in and connection to* from the previous paragraph with the word *empathy*. Stories create empathy between people because they humanize a situation: they take any given topic and put it into a humane context and, in doing so, create empathy with the listener. Take the Holocaust. How can one begin to fathom the horror of the Holocaust? The answer: through a story. It's the story of Anne Frank that allows us to access and emotionally connect with the horrors of her time. It's that individual story that, I would argue, gets us closer to internalizing and understanding the vastness of that tragedy than the numbers and stats that define that period of time, in that place. In teaching these topics, it's the inclusion of stories that will create empathy between the student and the topic. Empathy is a powerful bridge to understanding.

What are you teaching right now? Transportation systems? Ecosystems? Sonnets? Imagine crafting an assignment that asks students to tell a story about any one of those topics that must contain, say, five facts, and reach an informed conclusion. The story could be presented verbally in under three minutes, as a digital story or as a written paper. The results will, most likely, reflect a new degree of time and investment that you haven't seen previously from that student or group of students. Why? Because the form organically invokes the student to create that personal investment in and connection to the content.

You can't tell a story about something you don't know. You *can* write a paper about something you don't know.

Figure 4–1 shows an example of a digital storytelling prompt that seeks to take advantage of this theory about storytelling. It takes the topic of the water cycle—solid, straight-up science content about which students could write a traditional three-page explanation—and asks students to work in teams to create a story about it. Consider the two options: a paper, poster, or slide presentation versus this digital story, which asks water droplets to pitch other water droplets on a water cycle cruise. Both effective. But only one will wholly reflect the personality of the creators. Only one will fully engage the creators. Only one will deliver a full slate of human skills. And only one will be a memorable educational experience.

---

**Figure 4–1**

## Water Cycle Cruise Sales Pitch

Humans aren't the only ones who want to go on cruises! Water Co. has published the following advertisement in the *Daily Splash*.

*(continues)*

*(continued)*

> To all water droplets:
> Stuck in your same old water cycle? Looking for a new experience? Come on one of our cruises in our top-selling locations! We offer water cycle cruises through backyards, oceans, cities, and more!

Water Co. is looking for a way to attract water droplets to their cruises—which is where you come in. Here's what you need to do:

- Research the water cycle and how it can interact with landscapes.
- Pick a water cycle cruise location that runs through at least one of the following five environments: a suburban backyard, an ocean, a river, an urban sidewalk, or a subterranean reservoir.
- Create a media piece to sell the cruise to other water droplets—this could be a photomontage with music and travelogue narration, an animation, a video, a commercial, and so on. Your team decides, but it must be visual: no audio-only productions.
- The sales pitch must mention or show various places you'll visit and things you'll see.
  - → The cruise must go through at least three location transitions and one phase change (gas, liquid, solid), ending in its original phase.
  - → The cruise must make clear references to the effects in climate, atmosphere, and landscape at each phase, as applicable.
- Put a time frame to this trip—is this trip one day, one month, one hundred years, or maybe one hundred thousand years?
- The sales pitch should be two to three minutes long.

---

# A Brief Deconstruction of the Educational Value of Storytelling

Bill Buford, former fiction editor of *The New Yorker*, writes in his essay, "The Seduction of Storytelling": "Stories . . . protect us from chaos. . . . Implicit in the extraordinary revival of storytelling is the possibility that we need stories—that they are a fundamental unit of knowledge, the foundation of memory, essential to the way we make sense of our lives: the beginning, middle and end of our personal and collective trajectories" (1996).

I love this quote. Five takeaways:

1. **"Protect us from chaos":** I think this refers to how stories humanize content and the world around us, providing us a way into ideas and people and events that can overwhelm us.
2. **"Fundamental unit of knowledge":** I really like this alternative pathway into defining a story. It's true! Stories are these compact structures that are literally defined by a beginning, middle, and end. And stories make an impact only if they communicate something meaningful. A fundamental unit of knowledge.
3. **"Foundation of memory":** This suggests, of course, for academic purposes, that this form of communication is conducive to retaining the content.
4. **"Essential to the way we make sense of our lives":** See point 1. But whereas that phrasing has us (i.e., humanity!) on the defense, this one has us on the offense.
5. **"Personal and collective trajectories":** This points to how stories connect us to ourselves and others. You know what else forges these kinds of connections? Music. Music: a universal language. Stories: a universal structure of communication. It makes sense.

As humans, we *process* knowledge and information best in the form of stories. Conversely, as humans, we *communicate* knowledge and information best in the form of stories. Storytelling, it can therefore be argued, is the most potent structure within which to encase knowledge—for the purposes of understanding, remembering, and communicating.

The process of creating stories—and this book is very much about the processes of learning and significantly less about the outcomes or by-products—also has clear, explicit educational value.

- Stories have structure. At a minimum, a beginning, with a hook; a middle, which leads to a climactic struggle; and an end, which resolves the conflict.
- Stories require research—data collection, interviews, reading, and observation.
- Stories require organization, collaboration, and problem-solving.
- Stories require explorations of voice and language.

While storytelling may be the oldest and most universal form of communication, it is also one of the hardest to master effectively because, like an intricate piece of machinery, it involves a wide range of skills. And the skills listed in those bullets—hardly an exhaustive list—are the exact skills our students need to thrive in the world ahead of them.

That's the micro. Let's look at the macro. What is the punch, the thrust, the impact of stories and our need to master this form of communication? Stories are a critical format to *catalyze change*. They are emotional and personal; they are universally understood; they are capable of handling challenging content with grace; and they organically humanize complex issues, thereby creating a bridge to authentic understanding.

## Storytelling Power

**Andrea:** Well, because I'm a reading and language arts teacher, [storytelling is] hands down the most important thing. When you think about our past history, that's the only way we know a lot of what we know today. There was no TV, there was no radio. The only way we learned what we know now is because somebody told a story to their child and that story kept going. And so I don't think that's ever going to change. I think that's how we teach our children, and those children teach their children, and so on.

**Bill:** If you know your content really well, PowerPoints are always good for visual aids and stuff like that, but the teachers that I think are the best at lecturing are just good storytellers. And I don't necessarily associate a PowerPoint with really good storytelling. . . . I can imagine a teacher who's just a really good storyteller, sitting up in front of the room with a whiteboard and a marker . . . and just with their storytelling skills, [being] able to engage a classroom of kids.

**Emily:** I place a huge value on storytelling. You know more about the students, whether I am telling the stories, or they are. And knowing more about your students—and it doesn't have to be personal things or private things—gives the basis of what you need to really teach a kid, which is a relationship.

**Alyssa:** History is just a bunch of storytelling about people's lives and what happened to them, so I think that would be really cool for my students to do it more in a visual way than just in textbooks or PowerPoint.

**Todd:** They're just not familiar with that process of crafting a story through a digital lens. I mean, they capture a lot of their moments on social media, whether it's TikTok or Instagram, but that is just a flashpoint—a moment in time—whereas with a story, they have to craft a series of moments to carry a message with a beginning, middle, and end.

**Heather:** Usually we are able to tell other people's stories, which is at least the beginning of storytelling, but to truly tell the story of what is happening to this tree, what is happening to this ocean, what is happening within this person's attempt to do this piece of science, what's happening with this piece of technology—to get to that true creative level, [storytelling] allows you to explore ethics, it allows you to explore cultural significance, it allows you to explore the ramifications of events. . . . We read a lot of science fiction because it's a way of exploring "what happens if," and so to me, all of those are stories. And they might be stories based around something that is entirely real; it might be a story about a person or a piece of technology or a what-if extrapolation of what might happen in five hundred years. They are all stories.

An example from the world's newly formative year of 2020: the tragic story of the murder of George Floyd. That story—and of course it's so much more than that—continues to ignite a reckoning with humanity's past and present relationship with systemic racism that feels unprecedented. That story changed society's relationship to systemic racism in one fell swoop. As a culture: there's no going back. And that is because of a story that wrestled an overwhelmingly complex and seemingly bottomless issue into a single moment of human connection and empathy. A tragic story that catalyzed change.

There's the story of a German youth name Felix Finkbeiner, which has resulted in the planting of over thirteen billion trees. The story of Malala Yousafzai, a young Pakistani woman, which allows us to access and emotionally connect to the global plight of many young women who want an education and aren't permitted that right.

The point isn't that you and your students should swing for the skies and change the world. The point is that stories *can* actually change the world. Which also means that they can bring about change to your community. They can align themselves with important social-emotional learning objectives. They work, as articulated by Bill Buford, in the worlds of both "personal and collective trajectories."

# Digital Storytelling Structure: Five Key Components

Most digital stories that are being referenced in this book aim to be between one and five minutes long. This academic structure is designed to be compact and disciplined; the efficiency of the form is part of its strength. If you give the students ten minutes, they will take it. And the results will most likely bore you and your students to death.

We all know the traditional story elements that compose a narrative arc. They include character, conflict, tension, and resolution as well as setting, language, surprise, and a hook. Here's the thing: in four minutes, there is not time to develop these classical narrative elements. You need to pick and choose. Think about it: you also will be hard-pressed to deliver a full story arc or a nuanced character in that short a time. So, while we still need to factor in these classical elements of story, the successful digital story tends to be selective about which tools are featured to be engaging and effective. Here are five tools that can help.

## The Hook

I strongly encourage digital storytellers to actively look for and create a story hook. A hook is often in the form of a question that will be answered over the course of the story.

- Why do trees have different textures of bark? For that matter, why are birch trees white?

- Have you ever wondered who came up with the name Albania for that little country just north of Greece?
- If one third of the world each planted five trees a year, how long would it take to plant one trillion trees?

In a digital story, students have the first fifteen seconds to hook their audience. They should use it to plant the mystery or seed the story arc.

## A Visual Moment

Digital storytelling is a visual form of communication. In their planning process or their storyboarding, students should look to create a memorable visual moment. They could create it with a special effect, a camera angle, or a location that is unexpected. The idea is that they want to create at least one visual moment that will have their audience talking, that will provoke them. And if that moment can be tied to the content (as opposed to a gratuitous insert of fireworks, say) then they have a very good chance of their audience learning from their digital story.

## A Sound Moment

The same concept can be applied to sound: encourage students to create one dramatic sound moment that will bring home a story idea emphatically. They can create that moment with a sound effect, a musical crescendo, or a sudden silence, keeping in mind that the absence of sound can be just as transcendent as the abundance of sound.

## Character

Later in this chapter, I discuss character building in more detail. But the essence is this: a character is defined by the decisions that they make. Characters are not defined by what happens to them. They are defined by what they make happen. Therefore, students must be sure that, to the extent that the digital story is a character-driven narrative, the character makes at least one consequential decision in the story.

## Outtakes

Students love showing off their outtakes. It reveals the fun that they had in making the story. It sends a message to the world that they are having a good time. Outtakes also reveal process to you, the teacher. They can show how hard the students worked offline in their homes over the weekend, for example. To that end, you may want to insist on thirty seconds of outtakes as part of their credit roll. Perhaps have them show something serious, something frustrating that didn't work, and two things that were funny—the goofs. In other words, direct them toward revealing the process a little.

Additionally, when other students see their peers' outtakes, two things can happen: (1) they will realize that everyone struggled and screwed up and (2) they will also realize how engaged everyone was.

# Storytelling Formats from Television, Radio, and the Internet

One of the beauties of digital storytelling is the depth of the narrative bench at its disposal. Television over seventy years has yielded myriad narrative forms that can be applied in the classroom. We are talking game shows! Realty shows! Sitcoms! Music videos! Sketch comedies! Dramas! The list goes on. It's pretty great. Digital storytelling in the classroom is an invitation to students to utilize their intimate knowledge of television, podcasting, and social media formats to explore curricular content. That is part of the attraction for students—it taps into their practically organic knowledge of these genres of storytelling.

Figure 4–2 offers a quick look at the possibilities of digital storytelling genres and formats.

**Figure 4–2**

## Possibilities of Digital Storytelling Genres and Formats

| Drama | Nonfiction | Other |
|---|---|---|
| Mystery | Documentary | Game Show |
| Private Detective Mystery | The Nightly News | Music Video |
| Police or Crime Drama | Breaking News | Instagram Story |
| Legal or Court Room Dramas | TED Talk | Commercial or PSA |
| Superhero Adventure | Talk Show—*The View* Model—Panel Debates Issues | Sportscast |
| Horror | Podcast Investigation | Animation |
| Young Adult Fiction or Coming-of-Age Story | Biography | Photographic Essay or Storyboard |
| Sci-Fi | Comedy | Minecraft Stories |
| Radio Drama | Sketch Comedy | Fan Fiction |
| Movie Trailer | Late-Night Talk Show | Pitch or Persuasive Video |
| Show Opening | Stand-Up Comedy | Weather Report |
| *The Moth* Storytelling Model | Corporate Video—Glossy Intro into a Company's Success Stories | Sitcom |
| Soap Opera | Moving Infographic | Parody or Mockumentary |

Where it gets really interesting and deeply relevant is inside the streaming world of Vimeo, TikTok, and YouTube. YouTube—the social media platform that also serves as a widely used search engine—presents content that is created by its users, the vast majority of whom are not media professionals, trained script writers, or cinematographers. One result: they have moved past the traditional formats that television has spawned and created their own formats. Popular examples include the following.

## How-tos and Tutorials

YouTube is full of efficient, visually pithy videos that take the viewer through how to . . . change a sparkplug, create a survey in Google Forms, or create a killer curry sauce.

## Vlogs

The video blogging, or vlogging, format allows individuals to relay personal information and societal observations in a casual style.

## Product Reviews

A subset of vlogs are product reviews. This format features popular influencers talking about products that they are trying out, from makeup to shampoo to tech accessories. This form can also take the form of a list or "listicle" that ranks their favorite topics in a certain category. Imagine asking students to create a product review of . . . a novel, a current global leader, or your town's recycling commitment.

## Crash Course Educational Model

The *Crash Course* format is a quick-cutting, highly scripted talking head video with graphics that aims to take complex educational content and relay it back in a casual, humorous, story-based style. This style stems from the YouTube channel *Crash Course. Origins of Everything*, a PBS digital show with a channel on YouTube, is another notable educational format that borrows from *Crash Course*. It features a really smart host—in this case, Danielle Bainbridge—diving into complex issues with the assistance of graphics to tell the story of global "origins."

Both of these YouTube channels, along with larger enterprises like Kahn Academy, have helped make YouTube into a seriously viable—and, I would argue, positive—educational resource for students. Hank Green, host and cocreator of *Crash Course* with his more famous brother, author John Green, had this to say about the purpose of *Crash Course*:

> Finding ways to get people to understand why a thing matters without saying, "Here's why this matters!" A lot of that is embodying the enthusiasm in the voice and perspective of the host. But a lot of it is also in the writing process: telling a story that is interesting. . . . Ultimately you want to tell a story that is like one long continuous story because ultimately what education does—in addition to a lot of other things—[is to] help you create a story about how the whole world works. . . . Each class hooks into that central story of our built knowledge of our world, which is like science fiction—in science fiction you talk about world building, and I think all the time about how education is a process of world building, in the same way as when you're reading *Lord of the Rings*. (Hobson et al. 2020)

I like this quote for many reasons. In particular, I like its perspective that we are all, as educators, contributing to "world building" for our students. That perspective feels expansive, truthful, and empowering. And, according to Hank Green, this is done primarily through stories.

But I digress. The primary purpose of bringing *Crash Course* into the fold of this discussion is to offer it as yet another narrative format that students can use in their digital storytelling explorations.

# Spirited Activities for the Classroom

What follows is an exploration of five engaging and educationally powerful narrative formats, each of which punches out content in a singular and expansive fashion: game shows, commercials or public service announcements (PSAs), vlogs, radio dramas, and podcasts.

## Game Shows

As a storytelling format, game shows are tricky beasts. The reason is this: the kids can get caught up in the rules, the explanations, the scoring, and the introductions of the hosts and contestants. Before you know it, two minutes of their four-minute presentation has gone by and no content has been addressed: it's been all rapid-fire rules and setup.

Another problem: whether to script the entire game show or actually play the game. When they are fully scripted, the essence of the format—which is intended to run like a competitive sporting event where we don't know what is going to happen and, most importantly, neither does anyone else—gets deflated. The whole presentation has a fake quality to it. These traps can be avoided, however.

## Keep It Simple

There are two very basic game formats that deliver curricular content effectively and are immediately familiar to the audience: multiple-choice and matching games.

The strength of the multiple-choice format is that there are opportunities to cover content around all the answer options for each question. Multiple-choice at first appears like it's a game only for facts, but it can be quite expansive, depending on the choices that are given. *That* is where you will want your students to focus: the other choices that can lead to new and interesting content.

That takes research. Developing a question like the John Lewis question (see Figure 4–3) insists that students need to find two other viable alternatives to the right answer. They need to know John's contemporaries and other civil rights acts of the time period, and they need to research the full story of the *correct* answer. For example, while the answer to the sample question in Figure 4–3 is A, if the contestant chose C, there would be an opportunity to inform the viewers that the first Black representative was elected to the U.S. government in 1870. The art of coming up with a challenging multiple-choice question is complex, and the more your students practice and realize that, the better the game and the more educationally rich the experience.

---

**Figure 4–3**

John Lewis, a seventeen-term congressman and American civil rights hero who passed away in 2020, first made his name as a civil rights leader by

A. participating in the Freedom Riders movement in 1961

B. writing speeches for Martin Luther King Jr. in 1966

C. being the first Black representative in Congress in 1965

---

In the matching game format, shown in Figure 4–4, the contestants are asked to match objects in two columns. This could be Civil War battle illustrations in column A and the names of those battles in Column B; capitals in Column A and country maps in Column B. Or, in the case in Figure 4–4, names of birds in Column A and photos of birds in Column B.

Figure 4–4

| | | |
|---|---|---|
| 1 Wood Stork | | A |
| 2 Swamphen | | B |
| 3 Mallard | | C |
| 4 Oriole | | D |

*Photographs by Kerry Michaels.*

This is more or less a fact-based game format. The fun of producing this game format is that it can be very visual. Pictures of places, plants, people, landmarks, galaxies, and mathematical formulas can dominate. Additionally, the visual element of this game allows one to compare and contrast inside of the category. For example, imagine comparing different kinds of writing structures—Cyrillic, Korean, Mandarin, and the Latin alphabet. What do those four samples of alphabets have in common and what, visually, distinguishes them? Or, in the case of the bird photos in Figure 4–4, what details exist in the imagery that allows one to distinguish one bird from another? This gets your students thinking in terms of habitats, plumage, beaks, coloring, and size. These are all biological clues that can stimulate discussion. (The answers to the game are: 1 = C; 2 = A; 3 = B; and 4 = D.)

Aside from these straightforward formats, copying from widely known and popular game show formats such as *Jeopardy!* works really well too. The point is this: the simpler, the better—that leaves more room for students to deliver and discuss the content.

ACTIVITY

## Questions and Answers: Multiple-Choice Takes a Deep Dive

To get people into the spirit of this format, consider spending a class where students are working in groups of three or four. Task them with creating one multiple-choice question about a topic you are teaching. Emphasize that the real work is around the answers that are not correct but could be. Also, you may want to require them to create wrong answers that are factual (as opposed to clever fictions). This should send them scurrying to research related facts and events, thereby expanding their understanding of the science, the history, the person, or the time period.

*Then*, have them quiz their classmates: They ask the question and provide the answer options, and with a show of hands, the other students answer A, B, C, or D. The team that stumps the most classmates wins! It's a game within a game. And consider throwing in a dozen donuts for the winning team.

## Make It Real

As alluded to earlier, see if your students can make it real. Then we get real emotions; funny moments; and an authentic dynamic that will engage your students who are making the digital story *and* those who are watching the digital story. The best way to make it real? A prize! If the students are playing for a pizza, then it's guaranteed that they will compete . . . for real!

### Cast the Host and the Contestants Deftly

The host and the contestants are the two basic characters in a game show: the drivers of the curricular content. Consider making the contestants teams of two. This is because watching two people debate and answer is more exciting than watching one person think. The very process of experiencing them making a decision has educational value. Having contestants working on a team makes the internal workings of the mind external. And that makes for good storytelling. And better education.

It's best if you cast a charismatic person as the host. The host role is an opportunity for select students to shine, to take control of the narrative—literally—and perform. You know which students they are. The casting of the host is a ticket to honing one's presentational skills.

## Commercials and PSAs

First of all, what is the difference between a commercial and a PSA? In form, there is no difference at all. They are both short stories that are trying to sell you something. In intent, however, they are dramatically different. Commercials are, most often, trying to sell you a product—cereal, medicine, insurance, or a car. PSAs are trying to sell you on a change in attitude or behavior that is designed to benefit humanity. That is the broad definition. So, PSAs can be about not smoking, not texting and driving, being a more active father in the lives of your kids, or ways to limit your screen time. All targeting awareness or attitude changes designed to lead to behavior change.

In the classroom, the value of this format is in selling a hybrid of the two: selling academic content and an attitude change about that content. I can imagine having students selling:

- a love of mathematics;
- a flower bed to help regenerate the soil;
- Chinua Achebe's *Things Fall Apart*; or
- the idea of putting Ruth Bader Ginsburg on a commemorative stamp.

In fact, almost anything you teach can be retrofitted to this format to great effect. Let's look at the basic narrative structure.

Commercials and PSAs are designed to accomplish two things:

1. Communicate knowledge about a product or a behavior; and
2. Persuade or induce the viewer to like, want, need, or support that product or behavior.

When designing a commercial or PSA, you are generally focused on three elements:

1. The knowledge or information that you want to communicate;
2. The outcome that you want from the viewer; and
3. The creative approach that will seek to deliver the information in a way that will produce the desired outcome from the viewer.

Before we start looking at the strategies employed by this media format, it's essential that the creators actually know everything they need to know about their product or behavior. One can't sell a product unless they know it inside and out (think academic content!). Then, students can start to focus on creating a commercial about it. But this all begins with their own research. Once they have this, let the following tips help guide them through the rest.

## Identify Target Audience

The students need to be really clear whom they are targeting in their commercial. We all know that twelve-year-olds think differently than eighteen-year-olds, who think differently than thirty-year-olds. They all laugh at different things and they all respond to different stimuli. If this is the students' first commercial venture, I strongly recommend that they target . . . their own age range: their peers. This is the audience they know best.

## Articulate Statement of Purpose

Next comes a statement of purpose: what are the students trying to get the audience to understand and to do . . . or think . . . or behave like? Once they have written their statement of purpose, all the other decisions should, in some way, support that statement.

## Select Primary Narrative Tool

Like all narratives, commercials have many tools at their disposal for delivering their message. Narrative tools may include the use of

- humor
- mystery
- beauty
- aspiration
- celebrities
- fear and guilt
- music
- surprise
- forcefulness
- honesty and authenticity

But unlike most narrative forms, the commercial is only sixty seconds (or less) and can afford to employ only one or two narrative tools. The students need to pick their approach and then stay with it.

It is often helpful to look at existing commercials on TV and to analyze them. Which ones work and why? Which ones grab their attention and why? Which ones offend . . . and why? As they do this, encourage your students to make notes of the commercials that most successfully engage them. Then suggest that they take that narrative tool that is succeeding with them and utilize it—rework it and own it—in the commercial they are creating.

## Develop and Create

The next steps involve the following:

- **Brainstorming an Approach:** How are they going to sell their product or behavior in a way that engages their target audience?
- **Scripting the Commercial:** They have a maximum of sixty seconds, so they must keep it simple.
- **Creating a Tagline:** A tagline is a final motto or phrase that is designed to be memorable or to punch up their message in a dramatic way.
- **Choosing the Visual Shots:** They must include shots that support the message and the script. This final step is usually done by creating a storyboard.

ACTIVITY

### Scripting the Sale of Content

One way to venture into this format is to devote two classes to creating a thirty- to sixty-second commercial script and four-panel storyboard. Working in groups of three, students are assigned something to sell. It could be the qualities of the mineral zinc; the impact of a certain Nobel Peace Prize winner on humanity; or the responsibility not to blindly share information before validating its truthfulness. Whatever it is you are teaching.

The students need to

- identify at least three important facts about their subject for inclusion in their thirty- to sixty-second script;
- develop a tagline;
- develop a creative approach—represented in four visuals and key words, designed to target their peers, inside of which the facts will be embedded; and
- write the script and finalize the storyboard.

At the end of the class—or the next day—each group reads their script in front of their class, accompanied by their storyboard. The class can vote on the best commercial. This activity can be a prelude to a more in-depth assignment where they will actually produce a commercial or PSA.

# Vlogs

Vlogging (blogging with video: vlogging) is a narrative format that, let's face it, doesn't feel like it meets any of the criteria of genre or storytelling. In fact, to an outsider (perhaps you, definitely me), vlogging can seem like a self-indulgent format that has the ambition of glamourizing oneself with the express purpose of winning enough followers to engorge self-esteem and make some money.

I am dancing around the truth there. But upon deeper reflection, I find that the format is fascinating and is, in many ways, a novel extension of narrative to meet the digital age. Here are four essential characteristics of vlogging, which make it a seismic digital storytelling format for your students because of its capacity to carry significant content and intuitively engage their interests.

## Story—Take One

Here is what a vlog is not: a nonstop talking documentary of the vlogger making a smoothie; flossing just so; dirt-bike racing; or cleaning the garage. A good vlog has a theme. That theme can certainly be about cleaning the garage, but the story being told needs to take the viewer on a journey with the vlogger in that activity. The goal is to get viewers to go on a journey with the vlogger, not watch them during their daily activities.

This all suggests that a good vlog requires planning. What's the theme? A walk in the woods? Discovery of the best ice cream in town? Looking for all of the plugs in the vlogger's house to gauge possible energy usage? A cemetery tour? And then, what's the journey or story the student is telling? And it shouldn't be what the audience wants to know. It's about what the vlogger wants to know. Here's why.

## Character—Take One

The driving force behind successful vlogging is character. This format leads with personality. The story that is being told begins and ends with the vlogger—your student. The vlogger needs to matter—needs to give the audience a reason to care about them. Needs to find a way to attract an audience to them. The format is driven by viewers who emotionally identify with the vlogger. Once that bond is established, the interests of the vlogger become the interests of the viewer.

And this is where it gets interesting for you, the educator. Vlogging is a form of self-exploration. Vlogging requires the student to put themselves out there. That is not for everyone, of course. But for some, this format can be the chance they have been waiting for to open up their universe. Or, less dramatically, a small, healthy push toward confidence.

Another angle: For kids who don't think that they matter—have never been asked to articulate why they matter—there is an opportunity in this popular format. Vlogging asks them to turn the camera on themselves, in a setting of their choosing, and essentially talk, unscripted. The opportunity here: to give permission to kids to be like the vloggers that they watch and follow, and to see if the shoe fits.

## Story—Take Two

As with most storytelling formats, the next level beyond theme and journey are the details of the story itself. The beginning, middle, and end; the obstacles and the climaxes. Vlogging is no different and is in fact, perhaps, harder because vlogging asks your student to find the microstory in their daily activities: putting on makeup, working out, making an omelet, walking the dog around the neighborhood . . . and making up stories about your neighbors. This is tricky.

Two points: This is a good activity to get the students to dig into the very nature of storytelling and what makes a good and engaging story.

And here's the other superimportant thing about vlogs: they are designed for the students' selves and their peers. Vlogs are not designed for you, the teacher, or a general audience. This is, essentially, a peer-to-peer storytelling format. What other storytelling format out there can meet *that* criterion? Vlogs make the work less abstract and more relevant. That makes students more accountable for their work. That makes the learning deeper. They could create a vlog about their favorite book and why they connect. Create a vlog about that strange statue of Lord Hugh What's-His-Name in the center of town. Create a vlog about the most extraordinary spider web that they found in their backyard. Ready? Go.

## Character—Take Two

Here is perhaps the most attractive part about vlogging, for the audience: the behind-the-scenes aspect. There are two important elements to this intimacy. Vlogging features supposedly real people in the recesses of their homes, where only a few intimate friends are ever allowed. The bedroom. The basement. The kitchen. The backyard. Even the bathroom. The visual intimacy of a vlog is important: you learn about the person just by seeing the pillows on their bed and the posters on their walls.

The second is that vlogs are unscripted. Natural. Just shooting the breeze. Saying whatever is in your head. This unvarnished quality communicates vulnerability, intimacy, trust, and honesty. Of course, much of all this is actually staged. But only to a certain extent: the audience will see right through too much artifice.

The point is that the deep attraction to this form of storytelling is its connection with our daily truths, all of which further reinforces the audience's emotional connection to the vlogger. It's powerful. And it's risky. I wouldn't recommend forcing students to vlog. There's too much possible personal exposure. But as a digital storytelling option, it is a uniquely engaging choice that can deliver on (1) increased self-awareness and confidence; (2) curricular content; and (3) storytelling and digital literacy skills.

ACTIVITY

## Backyard Vlogging

One human skill that vlogging delivers better than any other narrative format is this: extemporaneous speaking. For academic purposes, vlogging is a way to get students to practice their extemporaneous speaking skills in a relatively unthreatening way. Unthreatening because (1) this isn't public—it's video that does not have to be posted—and (2) this isn't a format being forced on them by Shakespeare or NPR's *The Moth:* this is their form of storytelling—they invented it, they own it, so they can inhabit it.

Here's an idea to get this going. Have students pick a scientific, historical, or literary object in their home or backyard and create a ninety-second vlog about it. The options for the students range from mold, a composting pile, dandelions, or ladybugs (STEAM); to house history, trophy collection, rock wall, oak tree (history); to library of books, words on the walls, porch or yard as literary setting, figurines, soldiers, or stuffed animals as characters (language arts).

Students need to make it personal and vlog-style. The content needs to involve some real science, historical research, or literary imagination. It can't be scripted.

Go.

# Radio Dramas

The radio drama is a genre of storytelling that has a long history, often championed in the English-speaking world by the BBC. Now this form is back in the public eye mostly through popular podcasts that present detailed serialized stories that are fictional and dramatic. In Chapter 2, we discussed the key elements in the universe of sound, and they include ambient and natural sounds, sound effects and Foley, and music. Here, we want to focus on the *application* of these elements to create a story.

The radio drama format is super compelling for your students for two reasons:

1. Audio stories are, quite simply, twice as easy to create and produce as video stories. Audio stories don't have the demands of storyboarding, location shooting, visual editing, and so on. The whole thing can be done in a closet or bathroom (both of which can support great acoustics), for starters!
2. Radio dramas in particular tend toward the overly dramatic—that is in the DNA of the format—and students love to exaggerate and wallow in histrionic storytelling. That's often in their DNA too!

Here's the primary aim in radio dramas: to transport the listener's interior mind into a cleanly articulated visual space, populated with easily imagined characters, through sound. That's right: you want students to create a visually concrete world with solely nonvisual tools. The tools with which they have to do this are just sounds: verbal and nonverbal sounds. Here are just a few ways that this format can carry curricular content.

- **STEAM:** A radio drama about a climate change–induced disaster or a human-induced disaster—think oil spills. A problem-solving radio drama that is based on a mathematical word problem. A chemistry experiment gone wrong: what went wrong and how do we fix it?! Or, more imaginatively, a radio drama that features a bunch of white blood cells that must suddenly go on the attack!
- **Language Arts:** Take two characters from a novel and place them in a new threatening scenario (Harry and Hermione get imprisoned in Snape's mind). Have the students write out this new scene and record it, staying close to the original authorial style. Or, take a spare graphic novel or short story that you are studying and have your students reconceive it as a radio drama. Or, as an exercise in creative writing and audio cognizance, have them create an original short radio drama about a topic from your fictional or nonfictional reading syllabus—systemic racism, gender identity, immigration, coming of age. Similarly, they could create a three-character radio drama in the style of an author you are studying. Imagine the different stories you would get if the models were Junot Díaz, Edgar Allan Poe, Isabel Allende, and Richard Wright.
- **History:** Students can recreate key historical moments in a radio drama. These can be real moments that are well documented, or behind-the-scenes, closed-door moments where the students need to imagine the conversations between this and that world power to achieve peace. History is made up of many mysteries, resolved and unresolved. Have them pick a mystery and tell the story.

Creating audio digital stories demands that students focus on a few key audio tools. Here are a few ideas to help your students get started.

## Creating *Character* Through Voice

The majority of the listening experience will be taken up with one particular kind of sound: the voice. To create an engaging and effective radio drama, the quality and tone of the voices need to be in the forefront of the creators' minds. It's an easy thing to overlook. Students tend to just cast their best friends. But, just as in a painting one wouldn't settle for the colors nearest you, so too in a radio drama: the choice of voices should be, to the extent possible, deliberate.

- Listeners should be able to picture the character in their heads based on (1) the sound of their voice and (2) the words the character speaks.
- When creating characters, have students experiment with voices first. They should try exaggerating those voices. Exaggeration can often lead to succinct and engaging characterizations for the listener.
- Have your students ask a friend to close their eyes, listen to the proposed character voice, and then describe the kind of person they are picturing in their minds. They should do this experiment with several friends.
- Voices, in this particular format, work most powerfully when they contrast with each other. If the idea is to conjure up a variety of human characters, then the voices need to be overtly distinct in pitch, tone, pacing, accent, and volume.

## Creating *Place* Through Ambient and Natural Sounds

Students communicate place or setting through ambient or natural sound. If they don't locate the story in the listener's imagination—pinpoint a setting that the listener can conjure in a split second—then the story can lose its structure. And the students will lose their audience. Sound creates place.

- For example, is the story set outside? Where? Do we hear crickets in a country or cars in New York City? If the action is near water, do we hear lapping waves? A train coming? We need to hear that engine slowly approaching, getting louder and louder. Sound sets the story.
- Tell your students not to be afraid of overproducing—adding on layers of urban or tropical sounds that oversell the reality of the place being depicted. When one is limited to only one sense—sound—then you sometimes have to overreach in order to safely shape the imagination of the listeners.

## Creating *Place* Through Writing

Another tool to help define place is writing style. Students will want to write more visually than they normally would. The idea is to give the listener as many clues to the visual world as they reasonably can. A narrator may point to visual details about "the dusty pictures hanging crooked on the peeling wallpapered walls" or "the street corner animated by blowing coffee cup lids and paper straw coverings in small wind eddies." It's an actively visual form of writing that can focus students' creative writing skills while delivering story effectively inside of this medium.

## Creating *Action* and *Movement* Through Sound Effects

If the story has a scuffle in it, then it needs to sound like a scuffle. If the story has someone walking over cobblestones with high heels, then the story needs to sound like high heels over cobblestones. If the character is in an empty church—an ambient tone that can't be replicated except inside a cavernous empty church—and a door opens and slams, echoing around the walls, students should go and grab those sounds. Audio stories lead with sound; they lead with very specific sounds that are often emphatically placed to suggest action and movement.

- Anything that students can record themselves, they should try. The sound will be more authentic . . . and the production process will be more fun.
- If they can't record the sound themselves—they need a railroad horn, for example, and don't have one around—then they can find one on the internet. Royalty-free sound effects libraries abound.
- Be careful: In my experience, sound effects should be used sparingly and selectively. Too many effects will distract the listener and will, paradoxically, slow the pace of the action.

## Creating *Emotional Connection* Through Music

Adding background music to a radio drama is the primary way to set the emotional tone of the radio play. It can also foreshadow or punctuate a scene, as in a short musical sting that ends a scene on an upbeat, downbeat, or foreboding note.

Tell students that like the use of sound effects, they should be sure the music is there to serve the story—to help shape the emotional arc of the story in the listener's mind and not to draw attention to itself.

ACTIVITY

## Crafting Curricular Voice Through Short Monologues

One way into this format is through the creation of a short monologue—a gorgeous dramatic structure designed to humanize curricular content. Three steps:

1. Choose the topic students will be exploring. The character will be talking about whatever it is you are studying. Voting rights. The solar system. The extraordinary powers of red blood cells. One of the newest countries in the world: South Sudan. The latest work by an author you are reading. . . .
2. Have students choose three key character elements that relate to (1) the time period; (2) gender, ethnicity, and age; and (3) interest in the subject. So, for voting rights . . . is this character a young woman who doesn't favor women's right to vote in 1878, when the first amendment for women's right to vote was introduced to Congress? Or is it a young Black man who has just turned eighteen and can't wait to vote, in the here and now?
3. Have students put the two together. They should choose three important ideas about which they are going to communicate and match those ideas to the character they have created. Then, they can manufacture the voice through scripting and rehearsals and let the voice, the character, come to life.

These should be short monologues, about forty-five seconds. They can be delivered in class or recorded. If recorded, the students have the option of casting someone other than themselves to be the voice of their character, as a way for them to experiment with the power of voice. The aim: get students comfortable with exploring characters and voices—personalized perspectives—as a way into understanding challenging content.

# Podcasts

Podcasts are a fascinating and ever more popular form of audio storytelling. Their popularity arises partially from their mobility: people can plug into a podcast while on the move—driving, walking, running, tai chi–ing—anywhere, anytime.

But they also strike a chord that is unique in media. They trade in being intimate, personal, and authentic: tales and investigations coming from everyday people who have a reason to amplify their voice and share their experiences. They aren't designed to be slickly produced. In fact, they often sound like they were recorded in your friend's closet, creating a shared, private audio space: the podcasters and you. (In this way, they resemble vlogs: it's perhaps no sociological coincidence that both of these formats came to the fore at about the same time: the first decade of the twenty-first century.)

Podcasts succeed by locking you into the voices of the narrators and the subjects of the story. There are no attention-grabbing camera shots or explanatory captions to complicate the story. It's just the voice, the sounds, and the music. These are your primal tools to create impact. These are the tools you have to ignite the imagination of your listener. And of these, for the podcasting universe, the most important is the voice.

## The Voice

The voice in a podcast shapes the entire universe of the narrative for the listener. Consider the different voices that you have experienced that speak to a variety of narrative formats. The game show host. The NPR newscaster. The sportscaster. The talk radio gusher. Siri.

It's the voice that pulls you in or casts you out. But with podcasts, in particular, there is an ephemeral quality to this idea of voice that demands attention. That quality is *trust*. To enjoy and listen to an entire podcast, you need to trust the voice telling that story. This is not necessarily the case with other media, where the narrative source is not always apparent. But here, it is. Go to your favorite podcasts and listen hard to the quality of their voices. Those voices communicate the following:

- I know what I am talking about;
- I am a totally cool individual and we'd be friends if we actually knew each other; and
- have I got a story for you.

In this medium and format, in order to earn the trust of the audience, the voice of the storytellers should have common ground with the target audience. If trust is not effectively established within the first twenty seconds of the story, the listener will most likely tune out.

## Podcasting Formats

There are four basic formats for podcasting. Each form is designed to be repeatable in the sense that the listener knows what will happen in each episode. It's just the topic or theme that changes. These are the four basic formats:

1. **The Interview:** A student personality interviews different . . . teachers, community cultural players, entrepreneurs, farmers . . . every week. One poignant example is *Come Through with Rebecca Carroll*, which is a collection of fifteen "essential conversations about race in a pivotal year for America" (WNYC Studios n.d.).
2. **The Monologue:** A student comments on the local, regional, or national political or cultural state of affairs. This format usually comes from a well-known personality whose interests, perspectives, command of language, and insights we have learned to trust. *Anything Goes with Emma Chamberlain* is one example of a YouTuber-gone-podcaster; here Emma extemporaneously talks about her life as a nineteen-year-old.
3. **The Conversation:** Two students, in a casual setting, discuss or review . . . video games, movies or television series, food, or what's trending online. Or the conversation can cover a day in history; books recently read; different local ecosystems. A moving example of this format is *Dear Hank and John*, which features the Green brothers talking about stuff from freeloading roommates to what happens to bankrupt cemeteries.
4. **The Nonfiction Story or Investigation:** This format is usually serialized, and it is designed to resolve a mystery or shed light on how we live. It's fundamentally journalism for the radio that is deliberately reconceived as a story. The perfect example that is well known in the United States is NPR's *This American Life*, which is described this way on the show's website:

> **Mostly we do journalism, but an entertaining kind of journalism that's built around plot. In other words, stories! Our favorite sorts of stories have compelling people at the center of them, funny moments, big feelings, surprising plot twists, and interesting ideas. Like little movies for radio. (This American Life n.d.)**

# Twain's World

A fun hook into podcasting—if students actually need to be convinced—is to focus on the audio element highlighted earlier: the voice. What follows is a passage from American author Mark Twain, titled, "How to Tell a Story," written in 1897. Read through the passage. There is a prose part and then an actual story or anecdote.

- Make copies of this Twain piece and hand them out to the students. Have students read through the entire passage, out loud, calling on different students to read various paragraphs. Now, you know what reading a passage out loud in the classroom usually sounds like. Staid. Robotic. Perfunctory.
- Make a note about this to the class after the reading is concluded. Bring to their attention the utter lack of character or charisma that they brought to the reading of this passage. They most likely read as if in a dentist's chair.
- Have students work in pairs to pick one or two paragraphs that they will re-present out loud to the class. The aim is to present this material as if they are . . . at an overnight or party with their friends; hosting a popular podcast that the entire school listens to weekly; or persuading their friends of the importance of this information. In short: they should create a voice that will attract their peers . . . and beyond. This can be overnight homework.
- The pairs can present just one voice or transform their selected passage into a dialogue. They can also pick and choose sentences they want for their presentation, creating a shortened version of the Mark Twain passage. The presentations should be no more than sixty seconds. Students can record their voices and play them back or present them live in class. Consider having students close their eyes while listening.
- After each presentation, lead a discussion to identify what succeeded and what didn't. During this discussion, make a list on the board, which will serve as a resource of voice qualities to inform their next podcast. This can be very subjective, so there isn't a right or wrong voice. But there may be qualities across the board that will come to the fore.

**The point:** students, through this practice, will heighten their audio cognizance and become aware of the power of the voice in audio storytelling. They will become aware of how the voice functions as a primary creative element in a podcast. They will focus in on how personal sound is. They will listen actively. And they will come away with a strong sense of how to utilize this primary tool in their podcasting creations. . . . And, they will pick up a thing or two about the traditions of storytelling!

### How to Tell a Story

by Mark Twain (1897)

I do not claim that I can tell a story as it ought to be told. I only claim to know how a story ought to be told, for I have been almost daily in the company of the most expert story-tellers for many years.

There are several kinds of stories, but only one difficult kind—the humorous. I will talk mainly about that one. The humorous story is American, the comic story is English, the witty story is French. The humorous story depends for its effect upon the manner of the telling; the comic story and the witty story upon the matter.

The humorous story may be spun out to great length, and may wander around as much as it pleases, and arrive nowhere in particular; but the comic and witty stories must be brief and end with a point. The humorous story bubbles gently along, the others burst.

The humorous story is strictly a work of art—high and delicate art—and only an artist can tell it; but no art is necessary in telling the comic and the witty story; anybody can do it. The art of telling a humorous story—understand, I mean by word of mouth, not print—was created in America, and has remained at home.

The humorous story is told gravely; the teller does his best to conceal the fact that he even dimly suspects that there is anything funny about it; but the teller of the comic story tells you beforehand that it is one of the funniest things he has ever heard, then tells it with eager delight, and is the first person to laugh when he gets through. And sometimes, if he has had good success, he is so glad and happy that he will repeat the "nub" of it and glance around from face to face, collecting applause, and then repeat it again. It is a pathetic thing to see.

Very often, of course, the rambling and disjointed humorous story finishes with a nub, point, snapper, or whatever you like to call it. Then the listener must be alert, for in many cases the teller will divert attention from that nub by dropping it in a carefully casual and indifferent way, with the pretense that he does not know it is a nub.

. . . But the teller of the comic story does not slur the nub; he shouts it at you—every time. And when he prints it, in England, France, Germany, and Italy, he italicizes it, puts some whooping exclamation-points after it, and sometimes explains it in a parenthesis. All of which is very depressing, and makes one want to renounce joking and lead a better life.

Let me set down an instance of the comic method, using an anecdote which has been popular all over the world for twelve or fifteen hundred years. The teller tells it in this way:

> **The Wounded Soldier.**
> In the course of a certain battle a soldier whose leg had been shot off appealed to another soldier who was hurrying by to carry him to the rear, informing him at the same time of the loss which he had sustained; whereupon the generous son of Mars, shouldering the unfortunate, proceeded to carry out his desire. The bullets and cannon-balls were flying in all directions, and presently one of the latter took the wounded man's head off—without, however, his deliverer being aware of it. In no-long time he was hailed by an officer, who said:
> "Where are you going with that carcass?"
> "To the rear, sir—he's lost his leg!"
> "His leg, forsooth?" responded the astonished officer; "you mean his head, you booby."
> Whereupon the soldier dispossessed himself of his burden, and stood looking down upon it in great perplexity. At length he said:
> "It is true, sir, just as you have said." Then after a pause he added, "But he TOLD me IT WAS HIS LEG—"

Here the narrator bursts into explosion after explosion of thunderous horse-laughter, repeating that nub from time to time through his gaspings and shriekings and suffocatings.

# Digital Storytelling Projects

What follows are detailed digital storytelling projects that follow three of the formats listed earlier: the game show (history), the commercial (STEAM), and the podcast (language arts). These originated as part of the Meridian Stories competitions, which are run annually for middle and high schoolers globally.

PROJECT

# Game Show: Forgotten Female Heroes

**History:** Research in primary and secondary sources of a historical figure; storyboarding; script writing; information organization; gaming development; human skills

**Digital Media:** Live action game show production and documentary creation

**Time:** Three to four weeks

## The Challenge

Understanding history is essential to creating progress, as individuals and as a society, but what if parts of that history were missing? This is a common problem when it comes to a woman's place in history; women are underrepresented or forgotten, yet their accomplishments are equally as important as those of their male counterparts. All around the world there are women missing from our history lessons and textbooks, and it's time we try to remedy that.

In this challenge, student groups will pick an underrepresented influential woman from any time period of their choosing (or as assigned by you) and develop a two- to four-minute game show called tentatively "What Did I Do?" that showcases who she was and what she accomplished. This video will be formatted in a game show style, in which they will record two teams of their peers (or family members . . . or teachers!) who will go through a short, three-round game to guess what this woman did. At the end of the game show, they will conclude their video with a short forty-five-second documentary-style segment explaining exactly who this woman was and what her accomplishments were.

The video should express why this woman was influential to history and why her accomplishments should be recognized. The viewers should come away from this video with a better sense of why history needs to be more inclusive of women and their roles. Most importantly, you want to encourage your students to be creative! The most successful videos will both entertain (keep the viewer engaged for the entire length) and educate (deliver significant content that will both inform the audience about the woman they have chosen as well as make the larger case for the full inclusion of the role of women in our understanding of history).

## Process

Following is a suggested breakdown for the students' work. It is written addressed to the student teams so that you can use this language directly with them.

## Phase One

- Begin researching. There are plenty of websites and articles that detail the accomplishments of many powerful but forgotten women in history. Consider using words like *underrepresented* or *forgotten women* when searching for information.
- As a group, pick a woman about whom you think you could create a compelling "What Did I Do?" video and who interests you—a woman about whom you think your peers need to know.
- Do some digging. Using both primary and secondary sources (at least two of each), learn as much as you can about who this woman was and what her contributions to society were. Make sure you understand her impact completely. Questions to consider:
    - → Does your research reveal a sense of her voice, her words, her character?
    - → Were her accomplishments and impact recognized and celebrated at the time or only retrospectively?
    - → Why is it important that her contributions be understood at all?
- Decide on the most important facts and stories about this woman.
    - → Teacher's Option—Research Summary: Teachers may require that student groups hand in a two-page summary of their collective research about the woman they chose, with full source citations.

## Phase Two

- Begin to build the format for the game show portion of the video. There are many ways to develop a game show. For this challenge, I recommend a very simple approach: The host makes a statement about this person, and the players—in teams or as single competitors—make a guess. If done correctly (i.e., you don't give them quite enough information), they won't get it right. In round two, you provide another statement and they take another round of guesses. For this round, the players should have, say, a 50 percent chance of guessing what she did. Then in round three, you give the final statement . . . which should practically give it away. The players answer and the game is over.

Example: The first round could sound something like, "I grew up in Germany. I studied molecular biology at Oxford University. I was very interested in gene mutation." Have both teams guess what they think this woman did, and if they get it wrong, continue on with the next clue. After both teams have had the opportunity to guess three times, reveal who this woman was and what she did.

While this is my recommended approach, your group is free to develop the game in any fashion that you like. Here are some additional game format questions to consider:

- Are there bonus rounds and, if so, of what do they consist?
- What happens if the players get it on one try?
- Perhaps the game isn't just about what this person did. What other facets about this person could be turned into a game that would yield information about her?
- The example I gave uses the first-person *I*. Is this how you want to present your forgotten female hero?

Whatever you decide in terms of formatting, keep it simple: the game part of this should not take more than three minutes of your maximum length of four minutes.

- Once you have decided on your format, what facts from your research will you use in your game show?
- Simultaneously, create an outline for your forty-five-second documentary-style biography. What new information will you include in the biography that is not communicated in the game show?
- Draft the script of the game show.
  - This challenge asks you to shoot real players playing this game. This is not a scripted game show. In order to showcase your game in the most effective way, I recommend planning to play and shoot the game at least three times so that you can work with your best take.
- Preproduce the game show portion of the video: consider what it is you are shooting and what it is we, in the end, will be seeing and hearing.

- Seeing: Decide where you're going to record (I recommend that you do not shoot this in a school classroom) and how you want the video to be shot. What props will you use? What decorations? People?
- Hearing: What will this final product sound like? Will you use music or sound effects to bring us into your gaming experience? A quick look at a few game shows on television may give you some ideas for how to enhance your production with music and sound effects.

- Draft the script of the short biographical video.
- Select images to accompany the short biography. This biography is not meant to be a complicated video; just select a few images or video clips, if they exist, that capture the essence of your figure.
    - Creating a storyboard is often useful for the documentary portion of the video. Attaching text to picture in a storyboard can make organizing this part of the final video much easier.

## Phase Three

- Finalize the game show and documentary script.
- Finalize the documentary storyboard.
- Shoot the game show video (several times with different players, aiming for your best take).
- Create a rough cut of the short biography.
- Edit the two video components together, adding stills and graphics as desired and finalize the documentary portion of the video.
- Postproduce the video, adding music and sound effects as desired.

PROJECT

# Commercial: GMOs—Where Do You Stand?

**STEAM:** Research; genetics; societal analysis; character creation; script writing to persuade; human skills

**Digital Media:** Persuasive, short-form video production and editing

**Time:** Three to four weeks

## The Challenge

Genetically modified organisms (GMOs) are experimental plants or animals that have been genetically engineered by humans in a lab using DNA from other plants and animals as well as bacteria and viruses.

GMOs have strong proponents. They tout higher crop and livestock yields; better-tasting, more nutritional food; drought- and pest-resistant crops; and the ability to farm on marginal land for food production.

GMOs have strong opponents. They say genetically modified foods are Frankenfood and represent a dangerous proposition. They point out the risks of relying on a food system that has potential for unforeseen impacts to ecological and human health, and they cite heightened allergies, potential risk of abnormal tumor growth, and even death among the trade-offs. They also warn of becoming overreliant on a few specialized products, compared with a more diverse, nutritionally complex food system.

GMO ingredients are found in 80 percent of packaged foods in the United States, yet most people are not aware of it because the United States and Canada do not require labeling that identifies food as genetically engineered. Is this morally defensible?

And at least forty countries, including the European Union, Australia, and Japan, have serious restrictions and even outright bans on GMOs because they are not convinced of their safety. Is it morally defensible to discount GMOs' potential for feeding a hungry world already strapped for resources?

In this challenge, your students will answer "Yes!" to *one* side of this debate by making a TV commercial for or against a GMO product of their choosing. Whether they choose the pro-GMO or anti-GMO side is entirely up to them, but their job now is to be convincing.

## Process

Following is a suggested breakdown for the students' work. It is written addressed to the students so that you can use this language directly with them.

## The Setup

Research a GMO product that is commercially available today. For your pro-GMO argument, make a 120-second commercial for the GMO product, as if the biogenetics company that makes the product sponsored it.

For your anti-GMO argument against the product, a fictitious anti-GMO group sponsors your 120-second commercial—a consumer rights group or organic farmers, for example. Identify your organization's mission and why it opposes the GMO product: what problems do you see it causing? These types of ads frequently end with some form of call to action. What action is your commercial trying to elicit?

In both cases, your commercial must (1) communicate clearly what a GMO is; (2) communicate clearly the biotechnology methods; and (3) articulate the possible benefits and possible risks of the GMO product.

Your target audience is a group of twenty-five adults. They have been brought in to participate in a public opinion study about GMOs. They have never heard of GMOs, so they know nothing about them. For the study, this group will screen both the pro-GMO and anti-GMO commercials, after which they will be asked whether they support GMOS in general or not, as based on the array of product arguments that they have witnessed. *This is the decision you are trying to influence with your video.*

*And*, there is one more requirement, regardless of which side you choose: your commercial must give your selected GMO product *its own voice*. That's right: include a talking, nonhuman representation of your product! Think *Sesame Street* and its talking vegetable puppets. Or think of a product that is represented by a mascot that is like the product! For example, the Pillsbury Doughboy or the Michelin Man. The role of this character in your commercial can be large or small, from a cameo still shot with a small speaking part, to the lead role. But the character needs to be there.

## Phase One

- Research what genetically modified organisms are and how they (1) have been used in the past, both successfully and with adverse effect, and (2) are being studied and marketed in the present.
- Choose one example of a GMO that your team finds particularly promising and relevant, or menacing and relevant.
- How is the GMO made? What are the original plants or animals? How are they modified? Explore the biotechnology methods that transfer the science into a real-world product.

- Detail the real-world applications and benefits of your GMO. What is the problem that is being solved? For teams taking the anti-GMO perspective, research the possible negative implications of your GMO and be able to predict and present the possible risks.
- Over the course of your research, be sure to also focus on your opponent's arguments. In order to be convincing, you need to be prepared to address and refute the other side. This is an important step in the creation of a successfully persuasive narrative.
    - → Teacher's Option—Summary Chart of Pros and Cons: Teachers may require that groups hand in a summary chart of their selected product, detailing its beneficial functions in one column and the potential negative ramifications in the other while keeping track of the resources that the team is using to support their arguments.
- Brainstorm how you want to visually represent your GMO product in your video. In addition to your script, what photos, video, graphs, and other materials will you need to define the benefits and pitfalls of your product? In what way can you give your GMO product a voice?
    - → Groups may use up to twenty seconds of preexisting footage in their commercials. Be sure to understand the rules that govern the incorporation of preexisting footage.

## Phase Two

- Brainstorm about the key ideas that you want to include in your pro or con commercial. Here are some questions and ideas to consider:
    - → What is the most persuasive and potent reason supporting the position that your group has agreed upon regarding your GMO product? How will you best maximize that argument? At the beginning or as a climactic ending? Remember, in this challenge your goal is to be persuasive.
    - → What are your two or three chief selling points? These points could become the foundation of your video.
    - → Anticipate the arguments from the opposing side and how you can address those in your commercial.
    - → Who, in addition to the character requirement already mentioned, are the voices and characters that you want to include? Scientists?

Possible consumers? Consumer advocates? Salespeople? Will there be interviews?

- What mood will your commercial take? Serious and ominous? Light and promising?
- Your target audience does not understand GMO science. What do you think is most important to them? How can you target your commercial to interest, engage, and persuade them? How can you visualize the process of creating a GMO in a succinct, understandable way?
- To help with this process, I recommend that your group watch TV commercials with a critical eye. In particular, scrutinize political ads sponsored by interest and advocacy groups pushing their candidates or agendas (you can find oodles of them online). Notice what works and what doesn't work. What ideas can you adapt to your own commercials?
    - Another place to look: the Ad Council, which is responsible, in the United States, for many of the national public service announcements that you see on TV. For teams taking the anti-GMO position, your approach may more closely resemble a PSA than a product commercial.

- Your group should now have identified (1) a GMO product that has a defined market niche; (2) the key scientific points that you need to communicate; (3) the key arguments that you will make to support your position; and (4) a handful of creative ideas from your brainstorm about how to visualize and verbalize those arguments for your commercial. Now, create a script outline.
- Draft the script.
- Discuss and map out with your team what imagery you need to tell your story. Oftentimes a storyboard is the best process for this.
- Preproduce the commercial:
    - Scout locations for shooting (if this is being shot on location).
    - Contact the people that you will need to include.
    - Research, as necessary, the still images that you will integrate into your video.
    - Create costumes, props, and other set pieces, as needed.

→ Prepare the logistics for the actual shooting of the video.

→ Rehearse.

## Phase Three

- Finalize the script.
  → Teacher's Option—Shooting Script: Teachers may require that groups hand in their shooting script.
- Shoot the video.
- Record the voice-over or narration, as necessary.
- Edit the video, adding stills and graphics as desired.
- Postproduce the video, adding music and sound effects as desired.

PROJECT

# Podcast: Paperback Parley—Talking About Literary Lenses

**Language Arts:** Literary character and theme analysis; information organization; extemporaneous speaking; voice development; human skills

**Digital Media:** Audio recording and editing, podcast creation

**Time:** Three to four weeks

## The Challenge

It's literature show time for your students! A podcast show, that is. The podcast's aim will be to observe a short story or novel through one of the following three critical literary lenses: the Marxist lens, the feminist lens, or the New Historicism or biographical lens. Students will discuss a character or relationship in the story with contextual evidence and analyze it through their chosen lens.

The goal of their podcast is to expand listeners' understanding of a story by sharing their analysis through one of the listed literary lenses. Podcasts are unique in their ability to be detailed and informative while inspiring the imagination of listeners. Encourage them to utilize music and sound effects to strengthen their points and heighten the listening experience. Be sure that they include at least two people speaking in the episode to add perspective.

Just like any other podcast, the students must create cover art and a title for their show. They can use this as the visual while their audio plays. Don't forget that podcasts—like good literature—are designed to both entertain and inform. So, students should do both! Puns, comedy, and creativity are all welcomed to entertain and appeal to listeners.

## The Lenses

Three of the most common and insightful literary lenses are the Marxist lens, the feminist lens, and the New Historicism or biographical lens. When applied, they reveal fascinating new ideas and perspectives that can otherwise go unseen. Here's a brief definition of each:

- **Marxist Lens:** The Marxist lens analyzes the social and economic standing of characters and how that influences their desires and intentions throughout a work of literature.
- **Feminist Lens:** The feminist lens analyzes the implications of gender and sexuality throughout a work of literature, observing the ways characters challenge or enforce gender roles and stereotypes.
- **New Historicism or Biographical Lens:** The New Historicism or biographical lens observes an author's personal life and the era in which the literary work was written to draw conclusions about creative choices the author made and why they wrote the piece.

## Process

Following is a suggested breakdown for the students' work. It is written addressed to the students so that you can use this language directly with them.

## Phase One

- Pick a novel or short story that you (and your group, if working collaboratively) have read or that has been assigned by your teacher. Read through the three literary lenses and determine which one may bring new perspectives to the story for yourselves and listeners. If group members are not familiar or comfortable with applying literary lenses to text, be sure to do some research on your lens and literary lens use in general. This will improve your ability to find interesting angles on the character(s) through your lens. Also, the better you understand your lens, the easier it will be to communicate your analysis to listeners.
- Next, determine a main character or relationship that you'd like to observe through your chosen lens. I recommend choosing a character or relationship that genuinely interests you; perhaps someone with whom you identify most

closely or, conversely, understand the least. The final podcast will benefit from your honest investment in this process of discovery.

- Brainstorm five main points to consider discussing in the podcast. For example, through a Marxist lens, a character who is perceived as weak actually may hold significant power because of their money and social status. Once the group has gathered five main points, gather two to three pieces of evidence to prove each point. Rule out the weaker arguments and pick two to three finalized points to discuss in the podcast.
    - → Teacher's Option—Outline of Key Discussion Points: The teacher may require groups to hand in a summary of the five main points along with supporting evidence.
- Keep in mind that this isn't about discovering a correct interpretation. This is about finding ways to open new pathways of understanding about a character and their decisions and, in that process, learn more about yourself and the world around you. Have fun. Don't look for what's right; instead, look for what excites and what may be possible as supported by evidence.

## Phase Two

- Pick who will be speaking in the podcast audio (remember there must be at least two voices) and begin to plan who will say what in reference to the podcast structure. Suggested podcast structure:
    1. First begin your podcast with an introduction for listeners (which should include an explanation of the chosen lens). Feel free to incorporate music and sound effects!
    2. Next, introduce the character(s) you'll be discussing with a brief description of them, keeping in mind that some listeners will be familiar with the book and characters, and others won't.
    3. Then apply your chosen lens and discuss what is revealed about the character(s) using evidence from the text.
    4. Finally, conclude with how applying your chosen lens changes your perspective on the character(s) and, therefore, humanity.
    5. Don't forget to sign off!
- Consider how you can make the podcast and its structure *enticing* for listeners. How do you want to rope them in? What's your hook? You can prompt

listeners with rhetorical questions to think over during the podcast or tell them you're about to reveal how the book sheds light on a specific pattern in human behavior.

- → Listening to other podcasts of a similar nature can help you structure your story. Here's one way to approach this: each group member (1) listens to the first five minutes of three different podcasts of your choice; (2) writes down two or three things that you like about the podcast structure or talking environment—about decisions those producers made to make their podcast appealing; and (3) with your group, compares notes and decides which of those choices you want to incorporate into your podcast.

- Draft an outline of your podcast story.
    - → Dialogue for the podcast does not have to be scripted, but it should be well thought out and organized. You can stage it as a host interviewing a professional; you can portray radio personalities who love books and are just talking about their favorite character; or, if the author is alive, see if you can bring them onto your "show"—literally or through pre-recorded clips—and have them talk about the character.
- Design your sounds. Begin to plan out what kind of sound effects you will use in your podcast and ask yourself how sound can help enhance your conversations. Does a theme song play at the beginning and end of the podcast? Do you play a short jingle or sound effect between segments? Will you use sound effects to assist your storytelling? For example, if you discuss a scene with cars, you may consider using the sound of a blinker, a car engine, or tires squealing. Utilize the unique qualities of audio to engage listeners and their imagination!
- Draft your script.
    - → Teacher's Option—First-Draft Script: Teachers may require teams to hand in their first-draft script for review and feedback.
- The next step is to pick a name for your podcast that the team finds relevant to the themes of the podcast. Remember that wit is always welcome.
- With the name of the podcast determined, design cover art for your podcast. The cover art's only requirement is that it displays the name of the podcast.

## Phase Three

- Begin recording your podcast. Before you do all of that hard work, though, there are a few things you should keep in mind:
  1. Find a quiet space to record your podcast. External noise can interfere with audio quality.
  2. With your chosen form of audio recording, test it first by recording people talking at the same level as planned for the podcast. Listen back and make sure there are no problems with sound quality before starting.
  3. Give yourself lots of time to record! Audio recording can take longer than you think. The podcast does not have to be recorded all in one take; you can split it up by sections, by who's talking, and so on. (It can all be pieced together in postproduction.)
- Once you're done recording, edit the audio as needed. Piece together the conversation and overlay music as well as sound effects. With sound effects at your disposal during postproduction, take advantage of its ability to make your podcast more than a conversation; it can be a listening experience!
- Once the audio is complete, overlay it with your cover art in video format—the final deliverable will be a YouTube URL—so viewers will be viewing your cover while listening to the podcast.

Please note that a link to student digital storytelling work that supports and complements the ideas and activities in this chapter can be found at www.meridianstories.com.

CHAPTER FIVE

# Making It Happen in the Classroom . . . Seamlessly

At this point, you may be overwhelmed with all of the component parts that create the machinery that is digital storytelling. There is so much value in each layer of the process that it's hard to imagine all these forces working together in any degree of plausible harmony. From increasing awareness of auditory and visual cognizance to the iterative processes and time management, the pervasive problem-solving to the focus on story creation through character . . . or through a game show.

A storm is brewing. You have all these skills that we agree are vital to the students' future success in column A. And in column B are your students: Puberty with a capital *P* and Adolescence with a capital *A*. It appears to be a tragically unfortunate clash of ideals and reality.

And then, place all of those fluid elements inside the rigid structure of fifty-minute time periods . . . and you have chaos. Heather Sinclair, a seventh-grade science teacher, put it this way: "The first time is terrifying. But once you've done it, watching students take ownership over it is so beyond priceless, that *it's worth the risk.*"

## Student Awakening

**Morgan:** So, one person really liked research and they did research. One person was an amazing filmographer, so he actually captured that piece. One person might have been better at writing. That's all they wanted to do. It was just the writing part. One person was really good at speaking, so that person would be the interviewer. So, it brought a lot of different people together for an end goal and [to] work toward that end goal, which I think is very, very important for students at this level.

**Ell:** But at the start of this [digital storytelling] project, one, who absolutely—teachers were completely challenged with him 'cause half the time he did not attend classes, he did not turn in assignments—he was the one student who, like, seized this challenge and he was all about it 'cause he loves SketchUp. . . . And he was incredibly creative and also very adept. So I was just, like, in awe; I would watch him create his towers and change his moat, and to me, it was pretty remarkable. He was so engaged. The level of engagement is so impressive. They come to life with it.

**Emily:** I can think of a student that was no longer considered to be ESL but had been previously in our school. And his project for the radio dramas—which we did in chemistry—was fabulous. Because the hands-on portion of making the experiment and doing the storytelling was much easier for him than writing an essay, for example. And [it] let his personality shine through.

Does digital storytelling solve this problem of engagement for the teacher? I would argue that it does. Here's why.

## Offering Multiple Pathways into the Content

As discussed in the first chapter, digital storytelling offers something for everyone: writing, storyboarding, sound editing, graphic design, acting, music scoring, researching, organizing and producing (i.e., controlling!) . . . the list goes on. The point: practically every student can find a pathway toward engagement that genuinely interests them. That makes digital storytelling extremely attractive to students, including those who simply do not thrive in a mostly print-based, analytically oriented academic environment.

## Working Digitally, Inside of Students' Native Medium

We have established over and over that the digital realm is students' literacy. They own it. It's not a literacy that has evolved over the last five hundred years, since the printing press back in the fifteenth century. Digital literacy began in their lifetime and is approaching maturity. Staying up to speed on that evolution is crucial to the success and, honestly, happiness of youth. And, as we have established over and over, it's a deeply educational process to work inside of this literacy. So, let them do it and engagement will increase.

## Making Content Your Friend

To tell a good digital story, you need to know the content. The more you know the content, the better your story. This has been discussed earlier.

But let's take it one conceptual step further. This construct disintegrates resistance most students have around researching content. Think about it. You're a ninth-grade student and you have to do a paper about the dust bowl. "Damn. How many sources is the teacher going to make me use? How long does it have to be? I have to come up with four causes for the dust bowl *and* four consequences? Why do I even care?"

Those are some of the organic obstacles that you need to work through and around: the perception that the content is the enemy—the muddy sludge they have to wade through to get to the end, at which point there is freedom. Digital storytelling doesn't work that way. The content is the material out of which their cool story is going to be made. The content is their ally and friend, which will allow them to create a really cool movie. This is a huge *V* for victory in my book.

## On the Phrase *Engagement Precedes Learning*

**Alyssa:** I totally do subscribe to that phrase because if they're not engaged, if they're not interested, then they're tuning out and ignoring it. My secret is I just try to kill them with kindness. It's a bunch of moody kids and they don't want to be in school; they're miserable.

**Bill:** Your teacher can be going on and on and on and there can be a video playing, maybe a PowerPoint going, you can even be reading the words, but if you're not engaged, so to speak, you're probably not learning. So being able to engage kids first, you're probably right about that, is necessary if you want learning to take place. Unengaged learning just seems like an oxymoron. It doesn't seem like something that takes place.

**Andrea:** I think engagement has to precede learning. Because if they're not engaged then they won't absorb any information. Especially with kids this age; they need to come up and write on the board, turn and talk to a friend; they have to do all sorts of things or you completely lose them.

**Darren:** I have to have a successful hook. I think whatever successful introduction I have that gets that learning fish to bite, that would be extremely helpful to me to drive whatever comes next. And it's like a magic wand. . . . What I liked about doing [digital storytelling] last year was that there was a little bit of a hook to get everybody. There was a wide enough hook. The competition pulled out my competitive kids. That drove them in the very beginning. The idea of using their cell phones and creating video—that hit the artistic kids. The research and being able to be your team's knowledge guru—that appealed to other kids. They are not as creative, but they feel that they can do a lot of information stuff. So, there's a hook for everybody on a wider spectrum.

**Heather:** Teaching is an art. It is just as much as about how you do in a classroom as it is what you are doing. It is a very relationship-based art. If you don't have a strong relationship with your students—if they don't feel safe, if they don't feel comfortable, if they don't feel interested—they are not going to learn. They can't learn. They have to feel safe; they have to feel comfortable—that's broader than this idea of engagement.

### Empowering the Student to Control Their Pathway to Understanding

See the first reason. It's repeated here because empowerment is a key component to engagement.

# Implementing Digital Storytelling in the Classroom

The execution of a digital storytelling project has no formally scaffolded process that will yield guaranteed results. Each teacher has their own style and comfort level with ideas like student freedom and independent initiative; control (or not) of the media creation process; and a quiet, focused work environment versus a more rambunctious, students-all-talking atmosphere. You need to implement this approach to match your strengths as an educator—to find the balance between your happy zone of classroom management and the frontiers of that happy zone where you can create new learning spaces and styles inside of those same four walls.

There are, however, a few documented models that are worth sharing that may help guide the process. These models have been garnered from teachers who have been using Meridian Stories digital storytelling in their classroom over the past ten years.

## Across the Four Weeks of the Project

As I noted in Chapter 3, the fundamental process for creating a digital story is research, create, develop, and produce. In general, I am assuming that students are working on digital storytelling projects for three classes a week, for a total of four weeks.

What follows is a sample of how to execute a digital storytelling project over the course of four weeks, using a project about Edgar Allan Poe as an example. It begins with the assignment shown in Figure 5–1.

---

**Figure 5–1**

**The Digital Storytelling Project (Summary)**

In this horrific challenge, student teams are asked to channel the deranged but deeply intuitive perspective of Edgar Allan Poe and bring it to life in a new scene of terror.

---

## Research

Students begin by researching the curricular content (see Figure 5–2). In all of the activities in this book, the process always begins with content excavation: the curriculum. For the purposes of this particular illustration, don't tell the students where you are going with this. To them, this is just a week of studying Edgar Allan Poe.

---

**Figure 5–2**

### Phase One: Research

- Read and discuss a variety of Edgar Allan Poe stories to acquaint yourselves with his style of storytelling. Consider the following:
  - → **Perspective and Voice:** He is often telling a story from a singular point of view. How does this affect our experience?
  - → **Tension and Time:** How does he use time—and waiting and patience and the unknown—to create tension, suspense, and fright?
  - → **Setting:** What do his settings generally feel like to the reader? What do you imagine in your head as you read his stories? Bright, outdoor spaces with fountains? No. What is the palette of his settings?
  - → **Language:** How do his characters speak? Are they generally urban or rural characters? Does repetition play a role in his writings and use of language?
  - → **Motivations:** Poe's stories are about people. The horror (and the redemption) emanates from within . . . people. What are Poe's mechanics for making horror work through humanity?
  - → **Genre:** Poe's stories are called gothic. What does that mean?

---

In this example, the work begins with as deep an understanding of the curriculum as possible. This can be achieved in several ways:

- Over the course of three classes in a single week, the students can read three Poe stories for homework and participate in discussions in class revolving around the literary elements listed in Figure 5–2, as a way to build their vocabulary around how and why Poe is such an effective writer of short horror stories.
- Or, over the course of three classes, students read three Poe short stories for homework. In each class, working in groups, they are assigned one of the

literary elements in Figure 5–2. In the first half of the class, groups work together to write one paragraph about Poe's effective use of that element in the assigned story. In the second half of the class, each group takes one minute to present their findings to the rest of the class. Six literary elements. Six one-minute presentations. Three days. Three different stories.

By the end of the three days, students will have a strong sense of how Edgar Allan Poe wields those literary elements to scare the hell out of the reader while opening pathways into the darker interiors of humankind. The content is understood. You may require that teams hand in a two-page paper that articulates four of the key elements of Edgar Allan Poe's style of writing and horror storytelling.

Now it's time to create. Imagine the looks on students' faces when you tell them that *now* they get to create their own short horror scene in the style of Edgar Allan Poe. Two things happen. First, honestly, the coolest thing ever! The students are engaged. Second: content is their friend. All those things the class has been talking about all week will be used—will feel useful, needed—to inspire and inform their creation.

Let's give the digital storytelling project some shape (see Figure 5–3).

---

**Figure 5–3**

## The Digital Storytelling Project (Full Description)

Read the following passage, taken from the Edgar Allan Poe short story "Ligeia." Select three words, phrases, or moments from the passage, and based on those words, create your own original two- to four-minute horror scene *in the style of Edgar Allan Poe.* After the conclusion of your digital story, the group must create a slate—a screen with just words, like a *title slate* or a *credits slate*—that identifies your selected story elements.

For example, a group may choose to base their new horror scene on these three elements from the passage:

corpse

repetition of the sound

startled me from my revery

Groups may add their own Poe-style horror elements to the scene. Additionally, the phrase *style of Edgar Allan Poe* is not meant to lock you into a time period or dialogue style in any way. It is, however, meant to indicate a certain style of horror storytelling of which Edgar Allan Poe remains the master. Raging zombies stumbling through the woods do not an Edgar Allan Poe story make! What characterizes Edgar Allan Poe's particular brand of storytelling? That is what you are going to want to unearth.

**Passage from "Ligeia"**

It might have been midnight, or perhaps earlier, or later, for I had taken no note of time, when a sob, low, gentle, but very distinct, startled me from my revery. I *felt* that it came from the bed of ebony—the bed of death. I listened in an agony of superstitious terror—but there was no repetition of the sound. I strained my vision to detect any motion in the corpse—but there was not the slightest perceptible. Yet I could not have been deceived. I *had* heard the noise, however faint, and my soul was awakened within me. I resolutely and perseveringly kept my attention riveted upon the body. Many minutes elapsed before any circumstance occurred tending to throw light upon the mystery. At length it became evident that a slight, a very feeble, and barely noticeable tinge of color had flushed up within the cheeks, and along the sunken small veins of the eyelids. Through a species of unutterable horror and awe, for which the language of mortality has no sufficiently energetic expression, I felt my heart cease to beat, my limbs grow rigid where I sat. (Poe 1981, 140)

## Create

In this next phase, the students focus on how they will creatively bring what they know about Edgar Allan Poe to life. (See Figure 5–4.)

**Figure 5–4**

### Phase Two: Create

- Study the "Ligeia" passage and choose your three story elements.
- Brainstorm about your scene. Keep in mind that this is a scene and not a whole story. You are looking to outline a moment that encapsulates the suspense and horror of an Edgar Allan Poe story that is possible for local production. Here are some scene elements to consider:
  - → How will you start your story: what is the hook?
  - → Try to limit your scene to two or three characters. Keep in mind some of the characters can be off-screen—only referenced—and still be effective.
  - → What are your devices to build tension?
  - → What are you building toward? What is the climax of your scene?
  - → How will you end your scene?
- Create an outline of your story. By the end of this phase, your team should have a sense of the design and key elements of your scene.

This phase is your second week. Working in groups, students now create an outline of their scene, which they will hand in to you at the end of the week. You may want to set clear markers for the end of each class period. As a language arts teacher, you will have ideas about how to approach this story creation process. For example, in the first class, perhaps you will advise students to focus on the ending—determining what is the gruesome thing that happens—and then in the other classes have them track backward, detailing how they got there.

## Develop

This phase is like moving an idea from two dimensions to three dimensions. Characters, plot twists, and settings move from inside the students' minds toward a physical reality. And in this transition, creative ideas will continue to morph and shift, as they hit the reality of a video shoot. (See Figure 5–5.)

---

**Figure 5–5**

### Phase Three: Develop

- Write the script. Ideas to consider:
  - → While bringing your characters to life, consider what your characters are trying to accomplish in your scene and what is preventing them from their desired goals. Keep in mind ideas that revolve around words like *denial*, *bravery*, *revenge*, and *fear*.
  - → Consider emotion and tone in the choice of your language: how does spoken cadence and word choice (as well as meaning) contribute to your Poe scene?
  - → Once your first draft is completed, read it out loud, several times, listening for moments that are lively and chilling versus moments that are expository and lifeless. Based on discussions, begin your second draft.
  - → Finalize your scene.
  - → Teacher's Option—Shooting Script: Teachers may require that each team submit the final shooting script.
- Preproduce the scene:
  - → Scout locations for shooting;
  - → create costumes, props, and other set pieces, as needed;

  - → prepare the logistics for the actual shooting of the scene; and
  - → rehearse the scene.

- Do some camera work. After a few rehearsals, your group should think about the camera's role in this performance. Using your camera actively can be important. If your camera remains stationary throughout your whole performance, you risk the boredom of your viewer. Play around with your camera's settings; take turns filming; do what you must to make your script and setting visually exciting. Things to consider:
  - → camera angle
  - → panning speed
  - → zoom intensity and speed
  - → camera location variation
  - → sound: how will you mic your characters?
- Before moving into production, begin to consider the sound design of this piece. Horror scenes often heavily depend on sound and music to assist in creating the atmosphere of dread and suspense. What music and sounds will your team use to help fill out the atmosphere of your scene?

---

## Produce

While this final phase is represented in just a few bullet points, it is by no means the shortest phase of the process. It does, though, require an altered mindset from the first three phases, where students are designing and imagining. In production, they are actually building: manufacturing and aligning the pieces to create a coherent story. (See Figure 5–6.)

---

**Figure 5–6**

### Phase Four: Produce

- Shoot the video.
- Edit the video, adding stills and graphics as desired.
- Create a concluding slate about the words from "Ligeia" that you selected to inform your scene.
- Postproduce the video, adding music and sound effects as desired.

---

In phases three and four, which often blend together, two major ways of working together come into play. The first points to a critical collaborative skill set that gets put into practice: the delegation of responsibilities. There is simply too much that has to happen in this very busy phase. Each team member needs to be held accountable for some aspect of this development and production phase. The team will need a leader or a producer.

The second: weekend work. Digital stories can't all happen during the classroom period. These projects—like any school project—will require a commitment of time after school, over the weekend, or both.

Let's take a step back. Look back at Figures 5–5 and 5–6, at all that needs to be done in the development and production phases. Study it for a moment. Don't panic.

Now, unpack, in your mind, all the skills that will be practiced while fulfilling phases three and four. In Figure 5–7 is a sampling of skills needed to complete this work.

**Figure 5–7**

## Sampling of Skills

| | |
|---|---|
| Organizational Skills | Collaboration |
| Time Management | Decision-Making Skills |
| Critical Thinking | Listening Skills |
| Problem-Solving | Adaptability |
| Evidence-Based Narrative Construction | Resilience |
| Iterative Practices | Creativity |
| Storytelling Creation | Presentational Confidence |
| Digital Literacy Advancement and Practice | Visual and Audio Cognizance |

Hmmm. The big picture begins to look like this:

twelve classes
sixteen human skill sets (needed for their future success in life)
deep exploration of literary content
high student engagement
shareable outcome for peers, families, and friends

It works. It's messy. But it really works.

That is just one model. Each digital storytelling project will require adaptation. But essentially, that process—research, creation, development, and production—will be broken down into one week each. If this is a once-a-week, every-Friday-afternoon special project, then give it the semester or twelve weeks. But a reminder: one of the maxims that informs this book is that digital storytelling *is* the writing for the twenty-first century and therefore needs to be moved from the realm of the special project to being a normative component of learning.

## Digital Storytelling in Practice: The Whole Picture

The following is a conversation between two teachers, one in Maine and one in California, who have spent time integrating digital storytelling into the classroom through Meridian Stories. Here are their conclusions about the five reasons to integrate digital storytelling into their classrooms.

### Reason One: Human Skills Development

**Matt:** A key objective in middle school (and high school, for that matter) is creating inquiry-based curriculum that allows students to perform open-ended research, and then have that research drive or dictate the student response. In our digital storytelling projects, supplied by the nonprofit Meridian Stories, the students did extensive research on their topics (far more than they ever did on other projects) because they wanted their video to be the best. Through collaboration, they discussed various ways to answer the driving question, and collectively chose a central story arc based on their research.

In addition to inquiry-based research, there are a number of 21st-century skills that are fostered, including collaboration, expository writing, project management, time management, and digital literacy.

### Reason Two: The Iterative Process

**Heather:** I would take Matt's point one step further. The single skill that I think is most important is one that doesn't have a consistent name and it's the idea that you are going back to do it again and again and again until it's what you want it to be. Some people call it grit, some call it determination, some call it the iterative process. As a science and engineering teacher, it's easy to link it to the engineering process and the iterative nature of engineering.

But outside of an engineering class, it's very rare for students to have an opportunity to do something, tinker with it, go back and do it again, then tinker with it, add to it, tweak it, take something out, move something around and be able to sort of live in that nebulous world of "I don't like it," "how am I going to fix it?" "what am I going to do differently?" and "what pieces are missing?" We rarely give kids the chance to linger in that realm of uncertainty for a little while and then figure out how to achieve a finished product. Digital storytelling allows this.

### Reason Three: Student Engagement

**Matt:** My 7th grade students get excited about digital storytelling projects for 3 reasons. First, they get to

## Digital Storytelling in Practice: The Whole Picture, *cont.*

work in small groups. The 7th grade age group is all about social dynamics, and the digital storytelling projects enable students to socialize in productive ways. Second, students love making movies. Their generation consumes media every day, and across a variety of platforms (social media, television, YouTube, etc.), so they relish an opportunity to create digital stories. Third, we set this up as a competition, and nothing gets students more engaged than turning learning into a game.

### Reason Four: Storytelling

**Heather:** Agreed, agreed, and agreed. But let me add one more element that increases student engagement: storytelling. If you go into any elementary classroom, you will see story time and storytelling and you'll see read aloud and creative writing projects. And you will see those pieces embedded in the classroom as an inherent part of the curriculum. Somewhere around middle school, we shift to all content, all the time, and we lose that creativity.

Kids are storytellers. Humans are storytellers. We have beaten it out of all of us by the time we reach adulthood. Kids want to tell stories. If you listen in the hallways on a Monday morning, it's what did you do, and who did you see and where were you and OMG, what do you think about that?

Giving students an opportunity to tell stories about what they are learning is incredibly powerful. Usually, we are able to tell other people's stories, which is at least the beginning of storytelling, but to truly tell an original story about what is happening to this tree, what is happening to this ocean, or what is happening with that person's attempt to use this technology allows you to explore ethics, cultural significance, and the ramifications of your topic. This is what digital storytelling opens up for the students—and it is powerful.

### Reason Five: Ease of Implementation

**Matt:** The biggest challenge in implementing digital storytelling is carving out a set number of days on the curriculum map. I use 2 days at the start of the project to get the assigned groups organized and settled into their project of choice. After that, we set aside 1 day per week to work on these projects in class over the course of two months, with very set markers along the way. And here's the biggest catch: I may not know how to edit in iMovie or work the latest animation app, but I don't need to. I just need to know history, which is what I teach. The kids figure out the rest.

**Heather:** Figuring out the digital technology is part of students' learning and they are eager to do it. Knowing how to ask the good questions and then encouraging my students to find the resources is the way we go. Then a lot of it becomes trial and error, and that becomes a valuable part of the process. The final beauty is this: they teach me about the digital technology. It's an empowering side of digital storytelling for teacher and student. My supposed "weakness" becomes a super power: the students are empowered to teach me. (Loera and Sinclair 2019)

# Inside a Single Class Period

In 2017, I conducted a study about the efficacy of digital storytelling in the classroom, along with my colleague, Dr. Charlotte Cole, the former vice president of research and education at Sesame Workshop and the current executive director of the Blue Butterfly Collaborative. Using Meridian Stories as our tool, we spent many hours in the classroom, which allowed us to put together this model for the pattern of work in a single class for digital storytelling implementation.

Here is the setup. The Meridian Stories digital storytelling tool challenged teams of students to create short video and audio narratives around curricular topics. For example, one challenge involved modeling the format of the YouTube channel *Crash Course*; a second asked students to create fully produced storyboards around central characters in the book they were reading (*The Outsiders*); and a third asked students to reproduce existing essays digitally using text, voice, music, and a few select images in strategic ways to reflect their understanding of the text (see "Essay Analysis: Taking Control!" in Chapter 2).

As part of our research, we observed nine classrooms in action. Qualitatively, we focused on elements such as the degree of student-led versus teacher-led interactions and the extent and quality of collaboration among students. We also looked at the level of student engagement, their on-task versus disruptive behavior, and the leadership versus other roles within given groups. We also considered the clarity of the goals for the classroom period and the degree of accomplishment and sense of progress.

There was surprising consistency across the different classrooms in terms of how the teachers approached this technology-driven, project-based initiative, allowing us to articulate a model that could be used by others: arrival, intro, implementation, and closing.

## Arrival

Students arrive and sit with their groups, often with the desks facing each other. Computers stay closed.

## Intro

During the first five to ten minutes, the teacher communicates three things:

1. Clear benchmarks for the overall project and the classroom period, as well as sign-off points and dates to match (These can be written on the board for the whole duration of the project or articulated verbally.)

2. A focus on a single aspect of the content for that day

3. A focus on a single aspect of the process for that day

The interrelationship between content (the curriculum) and process (skills to explore the curriculum) is a theme throughout this model.

## Implementation

The groups then work for the remainder of the period at their own pace. It can take five minutes (or more) to fire up the computers and settle in. The teacher wanders around the room—along with the ed techs if they are available—going from group to group to guide and advise. Their guidance is around content first, and then process and skills. Formalizing this—taking one round to be sure that students are exploring and representing the content effectively and accurately and then a second round to check on their collaborative, digital creation, and production processes—appeared to yield the most productive results, as based on our observations.

## Closing

There is a five-minute wrap-up to allow students to shut down and set goals for the next class.

## Examples

Here are some examples of how the teachers we observed put this process into action:

- In one case (the essay prompt), the teacher focused on delegation of tasks: which words were the most important (content) and how students might want to use color and music to bring more emphasis to the content (process). She presented this information as a series of choices for the students. It was a perfect way to start as it gave the students a few clear things to think about as they dug into their work together. And the choices—the decisions that they needed to make—remained all their own.
- In another class (the storyboard prompt), the teacher handed out a checklist that mixed content prompts ("Are you demonstrating character perspective?") with process ("Is there voice-over and is it used effectively?"). Guidelines and clarity of purpose are essential.
- In another class, the teacher adapted the Meridian Stories process into a checklist and printed that out and had the students use that to guide their working process.

Digital storytelling experiences will always involve a combination of independent initiative and guidance on two fronts: the curriculum and the processes involved to effectively explore and creatively articulate that curriculum inside of a digital narrative. This classroom management model empowers teams to work on their own while ensuring that teachers provide the support needed in both of these critical areas.

## Digital Storytelling, Practically Speaking

**Morgan:** The teacher becomes more of a facilitator, and so the teacher steps back and the kids really take on the project itself. There obviously need to be constraints, which is very important too. But in that mindset, the teacher is going to be the facilitator, and the students take on different roles.

**Todd:** My typical structure of the class is I usually deliver a minilesson. I try to limit that to about ten minutes. That minilesson is designed to help them for their work that day. Then I can sit with individuals or small groups and we can troubleshoot specific issues. It's more of a workshop model.

**Darren:** There were times when I was sweating. I was afraid of moments where administration would probably get after me for letting kids be in little pocket places where they could film in quiet nooks and crannies in the school. And not being able to supervise my classroom and not being able to supervise the kids down the hall: that had me sweating. But I definitely was like, "OK, I am just going to have to do this and if I have to apologize later, I'll take it for the team."

**Ell:** They have to come up with a shared Google document, which they share with me. Each person on the team would have different roles. So, they get to determine initially which roles they will be taking. [Picking roles] is one of their most enthusiastic pieces. After they read the challenge, one person said, "Oh, I am going to be the newscaster." And the other person said, "Do not put me in front of the camera." Another person, who was kind of the most quiet and reserved, really came up with the technical, fun things, which I think turned out to be the strength of their [digital story] in the end. So it's interesting how that gels and comes together. But yes, the first thing that they do is they choose the roles.

**Heather:** Using digital storytelling projects in a class has been most successful when I have had a fairly broad topic; the one that springs to mind is the topic of biodiversity in a seventh-grade life sciences class. That's a huge topic. It's incredibly important and it's a topic that is most well told through individual stories. The biodiversity in rain forests; the biodiversity in oceanic ecosystems; the biodiversity in deserts. No student is going to survive a learning experience if they have to master all of those different stories. So, it's a unit that lends itself to different groups of students focusing on different examples of a larger theme. And so, in those kinds of scenarios, adopting a digital storytelling opportunity lets students access their particular hook into this broader theme and it lets them demonstrate their knowledge of that in a way that is creative and unique.

**Tamiko:** If there's no chaos, then I'm not teaching well. There definitely is chaos. My room is not quiet.

# Assessing Skills

In the past twenty years, human skills have moved to the fore and been fully integrated into the regional, national, and global standards against which teachers often need to measure themselves and their students. But assessment of these skills—for example, how much more creative are you now than before?—is a challenge, a conundrum that I believe often permits teachers to skirt the issue and relinquish accountability because it's not measurable. Command of curricular content is explicitly measurable: the test, the PowerPoint, the poster session, even the video. Assessing command of the human skill, on the other hand, has no objective tool that can calculate progress.

I'd like to introduce a model for measuring—assessing—the value of the digital storytelling experience, which, as I have discussed, positively reeks of human skills! It comes in the form of a rubric that you can share with students and apply across every digital storytelling project you ever teach.

This model splits the assessment into four categories:

1. **Content Mastery:** This refers to the curriculum—the hard content that you need the student to learn. It's first. This is where you lay out for the students exactly what you hope they will understand.

2. **Storytelling Mastery:** Story structure, use of language, creation of characters, integration of content into a creative storytelling format: the assessment centers around the efficacy of the narrative vehicle that students created to deliver the content. I have devoted an entire chapter to why stories matter. This is where you can break that down into the most relevant component parts.

3. **Digital Mastery:** This is all about digital literacy. How digitally literate are your students? Did they experiment and play around with font sizes; editing techniques (the hard cut versus the cross-fade); camera angles; use of music; and so on? The inventory of tools and apps at their disposal is ever changing. Your goal is to create a student who knows how to navigate the choices and then apply those choices. *That* is the writing part of digital literacy. The tool of writing in the textual literacy realm is the alphabet. The tools of writing in the digital literacy realm are text, sound, music, and imagery, and all of the digitized ways that they can be combined.

4. **Human Skills Mastery:** This covers what you observed from their process of working together that is not inherent in the first three categories.

The inherent strength of this model is this: many of the most critical human skills, which are hardest to objectively assess, are situated in the middle two categories: storytelling and digital mastery. Skill sets that involve creativity, organizational management, visual and audio cognizance, and problem-solving are organic to the processes involved in story creation and digital command. So, those two explicitly measurable areas—story creation and digital command—become umbrella concepts for a whole host of skill sets that often feel less explicitly measurable. So, for example, if the resulting digital story is derivative, not visually thoughtful, and peppered with moments of bad audio, then you actually have a clear avenue to assess the students' capacities in the areas of creativity, digital literacy, audio cognizance, and decision-making.

Let's look at the Edgar Allan Poe challenge and see how this model might apply to that project (see Figure 5–8).

**Figure 5–8**

## Assessment—The Evaluation Rubric for the Edgar Allan Poe Horror Scene

| Content Command | |
|---|---|
| **Criteria** | **1–10** |
| Whole Scene | The scene is engaging and effective at eliciting the sensations of horror. |
| Style of Horror | The scene is closely aligned with the tone, sensibility, detail, and thrill of Edgar Allan Poe's short stories. |
| Three Story Elements | The three Edgar Allan Poe story elements are presented clearly and used creatively to propel the scene forward. |
| **Storytelling Command** | |
| **Criteria** | **1–10** |
| Character Creation | The character(s) are compelling and perfectly suited to the scene. |
| Dialogue | The dialogue is believable and aligned with Edgar Allan Poe's command of language; it reveals character effectively and serves the plot well. |
| Scene Structure | The scene is engaging and clearly well structured. |

*(continues)*

*(continued)*



| Digital Command | |
|---|---|
| **Criteria** | **1–10** |
| Acting | The acting is believable and engaging, contributing to the scene's success. |
| Setting and Cinematography | The setting and use of the camera support the action of the scene and help create the tension necessary to sustain a horror scene. |
| Editing and Music | The scene is edited cleanly and effectively.<br>The selective use of music and sound effects enhances the horror and drama inherent in the scene. |
| **Human Skills Command** | |
| **Criteria** | **1–10** |
| Collaborative Thinking, Decision-Making, and Listening | The group demonstrated flexibility in making compromises and valued the contributions of each group member. |
| Resiliency, Adaptation, and Iterative Processes | The group overcame frustrating obstacles through a process of revising and rethinking key story ideas and digital approaches. |
| Initiative, Self-Direction, and Time Management | The group set attainable goals, worked independently, and managed their time effectively, demonstrating a disciplined commitment to the project. |

You will note that in this model, there are three subheadings per category. While it may be tempting to create more, I wouldn't recommend it. That may overwhelm students. This model is designed to provide a clear set of project objectives for the students to which they can constantly refer as they are going through the digital storytelling process.

And here is the underlying message to students about the application of this assessment tool: content and process are on equal ground. In fact, they may start to see their capacities to master storytelling and digital creation *as content*. Which, I would argue, it is. But regardless, the message in this assessment tool clearly communicates that content is not everything—something a classic test does seem to suggest—and is in fact of equal value to these other skill sets. That is such an important message to send to your students.

### Digital Storytelling and Assessment

**Morgan:** Sometimes when I use digital storytelling, it's the end-all unit: that's the assessment. It's instead of a test or instead of a final paper-and-pencil piece. They can actually show their knowledge of the content. They can show a final product and very eloquently show their knowledge in a digital media format.

. . . When we talk about assessment, we are talking about content. One of the things in science that I am supposed to be assessing is how to be creative about going about a problem. If you are faced with a problem, how creatively can you solve it? It's that creativity side of "Can you think outside of the box?" Those are extremely important. Can you assess that? Not so much. Do you want to see that every day in a student? Absolutely. Is it an expectation of my students? Absolutely. Am I going to assess that [independently or in isolation]? No. But it's going to make their projects look so much better. It can add to mathematics. Can you solve this problem three ways? How creative are you about that?

. . . I think the hardest thing for teachers is to tell who did what in that project. That's going to be a hard thing for them to quantify. With that, I have self-assessments; I have questions like "What part were you most important for?" and "What role did you take?" and "Were you more one of the people who led or one of the people who followed?" and "What was your specific part that you contributed to this?" And I have them do a reflection on each one of those.

## Incentivizing Learning: Strategies to Increase Engagement Around Digital Storytelling Projects

Digital storytelling projects break the traditional mold of one particular tie between the teacher and student whereby the teacher is the only witness to the student's work. I am talking about when the teacher is the only one who reads the paper, sees the test, or reads the journal entry or the experiment write-up. While this structure has its purposes—among others, to protect the privacy of the students and their schoolwork—it also creates mystery and confusion: students often have no idea of their standing vis-à-vis other students. Students can exist as isolated islands floating around in a classroom, not learning from the successes and failures of their peers.

Digital storytelling projects have a public face—a transparency that is novel for many and a structure that organically lends itself to an audience of more than just one: you. And this intrinsic framework lends itself to some strategies that can be very attractive to the students and very conducive to a positive educational experience.

## Competition

As you may recall from the first chapter, I was the cocreator and producer of a reality game show in Iraq that targeted teens, called *Salam Shabab* ("Peace, Youth"). It was a television series that was sponsored by the US Institute of Peace and was driven by a curriculum that was designed "to create the foundations of peace building by empowering Iraqi youth to be confident, open-minded and participatory citizens of a diverse society."

I learned many things from that incredible experience. One of them was this: competition, as a motivational force, works extremely well if you place youth in a safe, friendly, and supportive environment. Competitions *don't* work well when the value of the reward at the end outweighs the value of the competitive process itself.

I will cut to a sports analogy to help make sense of this. The coach who just wants to win will fail. We know that. They will fail their student athletes, who will buckle under the pressure of the prominence of the final goal. But the coach who is coaching for the love of the game—the process—while still aiming to win, of course, is the one under whom the athletes will grow. That's the person who will bring out their best work. And so it goes in the classroom.

Digital storytelling lends itself to working in groups in a safe, friendly, and supportive environment—your classroom. Meridian Stories is driven by an annual competition: fifteen digital storytelling challenges—five each in language arts, STEAM, and history—due in the spring of every school year. Why? Because I trust school environments to leverage the incentive of competitions—something to which most young people, in some manner, respond—to create a motivational atmosphere that is supportive, playful, and rigorous. The prize for coming in first, second, or third in Meridian Stories is just online, public recognition. And digital badges are awarded in recognition of outstanding work in the areas of content, storytelling, and digital creation. For your class, you might award them with a pizza party or some homemade chocolate chip cookies or offer a chance for the winning team to teach a full class or even skip one assignment. This is all up to you. There are no rules because we do recognize that competition is not for everyone and doesn't necessarily succeed at motivating students: it can demoralize.

But I would argue, more often than not, a dose of competitive spirit will increase students' accountability, thereby improving their work.

## Outside Feedback

The idea here is simple and effective: bring in adults who are respected in the field in which you are studying to provide feedback to the students on their work. The people could be

- other teaching colleagues or school administrators;
- local community members who work professionally in, for example, biology, media creation, fiction writing, or the local historical society; or
- the network of your friends, or perhaps one of your students' parents, who would be willing to volunteer a few hours to screen and comment upon your students' work.

The outside-feedback concept is part and parcel of the authentic learning movement, which ties in school learning to the real world. There are a lot of articles and research studies that support this framework. But for our purposes, the logic is simple: when students receive validation from (1) someone other than the teacher and (2) someone in a professional field that is not education and therefore brings a "professional" lens to the work, the validation feels exponentially more valuable.

I don't have scientific proof of that. That statement is based on my experience in this realm. But it makes sense. Here's what one eighth-grade student wrote upon receiving comments from the judges in a Meridian Stories competition:

> **"It was so amazing to receive detailed, meaningful positive feedback from the mentors on my work. After reading it I jumped up and down. It made me very happy to read their reviews on the project. I was excited to have these suggestions from such smart people in their fields to continue improving my work. In the future I see myself doing this again. In the end, thank you so much for sending the results, but more importantly thank you for giving this assignment."**

If you do decide to integrate feedback from noneducators, you *will* get people who simply don't know how to communicate to students in an effective way—it is, as you well know, its own art form. One mentor began her comments with the line, "*Star Wars* text scrolling?!! Really?" I shut that one down right then and there and submitted my own review to the student instead. So, be sure to proof the feedback before it reaches the student!

# Presentation of Learning

There is this nonprofit out there called Share Your Learning, which is spearheading the movement of having over five million students publicly share their work as a meaningful part of their educational experience.

According to Share Your Learning (n.d.),

> **Presentations of Learning (POL) promote . . .**
>
> - **Student Ownership, Responsibility & Engagement.** POLs can serve as a powerful *rite of passage* at the end of a semester or academic year [or a project]. By reflecting on their growth over time, grounded in evidence from their work, students are encouraged to take ownership of their learning in relation to academic and character goals. Just as an artist wants their portfolio to represent their best work, POLs encourage students to care deeply about the work they will share.
> - **Community Pride & Involvement.** When peers, teachers and community members come together to engage with student work and provide authentic feedback, they become invested in students' growth and serve as active contributors to the school community.
> - **Equity.** POLs provide an opportunity for all students to celebrate, reflect, plot a course forward, and ask for the support they need. They ensure that all students are seen, and provide insight into what learning experiences students find most meaningful and relevant to their lives.

My own research indicates this to be a really useful exercise for one additional reason: students actually learn from their peers' presentations; it is useful to hear a perspective that is not just the teacher's.

It is with this in mind that I encourage you to plan an event—it could be just an end-of-the-week class or an event where parents, teachers, and student peers are invited—to allow the students to showcase their digital storytelling projects.

## Presentation of Learning: Why Do It?

**Tamiko:** Excitement. Pride. That's the reward. It's a reward when they can come in, looking professional—'cause they all dress up without me saying a word about it—and they can walk around, show Mom and Dad the exhibit; they go right to their own and they wait for people to come and they will go up and interact, not wait for a parent to ask a question. It's all about their sharing and the composure that they have that they did this.

Usually by eighth grade, I have my kids present in a group that is not affiliated with the school. And that really scares them. If I host it at the school, that is still a comfort zone. But they are required to do a presentation, not in front of their peers and not school related. Most of them end up going to their parents' workplace and they get on the agenda and the parents film it on their phone and they send the clip over to me. That is about them sharing their work with a group that has no vested interest, no information whatsoever. But it's a way of saying, "You are ready for this." Because you need to—as much technology as there is, you still need those face-to-face skills. And we practice that all the way through eighth grade; now you're going out. They are so not happy with me, but they feel like a million dollars when they come back. They did it. The parents are so proud. . . . [The students] can feel that they are worthy.

**Morgan:** When the students do something for the teacher, it's good enough, but when they have to do something for the greater public, it's really good. So, it's one of those things that is like, "Oh my gosh, my peers might see this." . . . And that's where having an audience [makes a difference]. It has to be a polished piece. A lot of times kids don't get a chance to put a polishing piece of creativity on their own work. And this allows for that.

**Emily:** At the end of a digital storytelling project, the students share with each other and the class as whole and often with other classes. The value in sharing the work is actually a key part of digital storytelling. You want to have an audience. So, there is a huge value. One of the values I see in digital storytelling is you learn about things and skills that you might not otherwise see. Students give value to each other in ways that they might not have seen before. And that comes from presenting their work.

# Public Sharing: Creating Impact

To conclude this journey, I want to bring your attention to one more impactful avenue that this model offers up. Digital stories are designed to be published to a wider world; they're designed for an audience that goes beyond the teacher and perhaps the classroom. As indicated previously, this is a form of narrative that is perfectly suited to be amplified in the participatory culture in which youth thrive. So, the last step in this—and this is certainly after you have successfully integrated digital storytelling activities into your classroom several times—is to encourage your students to publish their work. This can be especially powerful if you set this up as a challenge to research, create, develop, and produce a digital story that is intended to create an impact of some kind, locally or nationally.

Because within this digital universe, there are multiple opportunities to measure that impact with the data and metrics one can easily access inside of the various social media platforms. This is an unprecedented circumstance in education: accessing the existing digital mechanisms that allow students to actually make a difference while they are still secondary students. No advanced degrees required!

Here are a few questions to ask of the students that can help launch your students' work into the massive digital dialogue that is taking place in the world.

- Who is your audience? How will you tag your work to reach the widest available audience?
- What are your objectives? Is your story a call to action? A persuasive story? A story intended to increase awareness or deliver knowledge?
- What do you hope people will feel or do as a result of seeing or listening to your story? Is there a way to measure that?
- What are the easiest digital platforms via which to reach your target audience? Consider editing together a short trailer for those platforms that will further engage your audience in your work.
- In terms of reach, how will you measure the success of sharing your work?
- Is your sharing mechanism designed to allow others to share it more widely?

# Concluding . . . at the Starting Gate

There is, perhaps, an overwhelming number of activities and perspectives emanating from this book. As stated at the start of this book, if you were to include them all in order to build this literacy to its full potential—to make it feel like an organic and effortless form of communication for your students—then I suspect your carefully curated classroom planning would be upended. That is not the purpose of this book.

If you do believe that digital storytelling is indeed writing for your students—one of two wholly viable and daily literacies—then for starters, be selective. I would recommend choosing four to eight activities for the first year, building up to one or two full-on digital stories in the spring. Imagine planning a year that integrated these activities and projects into the content that you already teach:

- Sound Stories of Place or Your Daily Score (Chapter 2)
- A Story in Eight Pictures: Getting Personal (Chapter 2)
- Questioning Character (Chapter 3)
- Four-Frame Storyboarding (Chapter 3)
- Questions and Answers: Multiple-Choice Takes a Deep Dive (Chapter 4)
- Backyard Vlogging (Chapter 4)
- a full-on digital story—from this book, online resources, or your own creation

Does that work for you? Imagine a year whereby you were consistently experimenting with these various approaches to learning with your students. What do you foresee? From my very biased perspective, I see super amounts of creativity and high engagement; lots of presentational moments; and a deep investigation into the power of sound and imagery to effectively communicate. I see lots of experimentation with narrative structures and the many different ways to organize content in compelling ways. I see group work and chaos. I see humor as well—plenty of places for the students to have their voices, comic or otherwise, penetrate through the educational content, resulting in a blended subjective and objective narrative as framed by the evolving visual and mental mindsets of your students.

Here's another rundown of select activities and projects:

- Sound Creativity: Foley Bursts (Chapter 2)
- Essay Analysis: Taking Control! (Chapter 2) (you could add the Foley work and mix that into their essay analysis)
- Captioning Images: Pictures Versus Words (Chapter 2)
- Crafting Curricular Voice Through Short Monologues (Chapter 4)
- Interior Designing (Chapter 3)
- Facebook (Meta) Profiles (Chapter 3)
- a full-on digital story—from this book, online resources, or your own creation

In this sequence of activities, I have attempted to assign some order. Hard to see, I know. But the idea here is to move from sound to words (and mix the two) to images. And then apply this knowledge to character and setting, ending with Facebook Profiles, which asks students to apply all of this knowledge in one assignment. Then end with a full-on digital story assignment.

It's another approach to organizing and applying the ideas from this book into your classroom reality. Going back to the analogy that Hank Green spoke of in Chapter 4 about world building and how "each class hooks into that central story of our built knowledge of our world" (Hobson et al. 2020), the first rundown takes a random building blocks approach and the second, a more premeditated, sequenced approach. I think it's worth extending this metaphor to suggest that each activity and project is a world-building building block. You are delivering the content in an engaging and thoughtful way. And you are delivering the skills in a way that builds their digital vocabulary to communicate effectively with the world—to think of ideas and solutions and artistic concepts through the lens of . . . photography, character, voice, music, satire, games, podcasting, setting . . . and words.

# Digital Storytelling Projects: A Cross-Disciplinary Trio of Challenges

This is the end of my story of digital storytelling. It's a story that began with my son and his digital attempts at popularity, ran through a digital house of mirrors where everywhere you looked there were possibilities for engaging, fun, and deep learning experiences designed to build the capacity for your students to thrive and excel in the unknown futures that lie ahead, and will end here, back with my son. After recently graduating from Vassar College with a dual major in education and environmental science, he created, for his senior thesis project, a series of interdisciplinary digital storytelling experiences around environmental sciences, language arts, and history. The core element that shapes his life and, he believes, can profoundly inform students' understanding of their environment, societal history, and the powers of personal reflection is, *the river*. I have adapted his work into more formalized digital storytelling projects that allow the various disciplines of social studies, language arts, and STEAM to work together to investigate the literal and figurative concept of the river in our society. Take a look . . . and make it happen.

# Healthy Rivers: A Call to Action

## A STEAM challenge designed for middle and high school students

This digital storytelling challenge is part of a cross-disciplinary set of projects that feature the river as a core element connecting language arts, history, and the sciences. Why rivers? Because rivers are one of the elemental ecosystems around which anthropogenic activities are being assessed. Rivers are also a strong symbol of hope and inspiration—a metaphor for the cyclical robustness of nature and of humanity. And they are pathways to worlds far beyond the classroom, across the globe and back in time; they're humanity's first transportation grid, which can be used to trace our historical expansion around the world. The river spans the realms of science, history, culture, economics, and creativity like few other natural elements in this world and therefore is an invaluable subject around which to research and communicate meaningful stories. For an overview of the activity, see Figure 5–9.

Figure 5–9

| Table of Contents | Range of Activities |
|---|---|
| • The Challenge<br>• Assumptions and Logistics<br>• Process<br>• Media Support Resources<br>• Evaluation<br>• Essential Questions<br>• Student Proficiencies<br>• Curricular Correlations | • Research, including field work (if feasible), on local river system<br>• Exploration of the metrics that determine a healthy river<br>• Interviews with scientific experts on rivers<br>• Creation of an action plan for the river's sustainable health<br>• Persuasive script writing<br>• Digital literacy skills: video preproduction, production, and postproduction<br>• Human skills: creativity, collaboration, critical thinking, and presentational skills |

## The Challenge

This challenge is designed to give students a foundational structural understanding of river ecology. It begins with the question: What makes a river healthy or unhealthy? And the journey to answer that question is a journey through the science of river ecosystems, climate change, and the anthropogenic threats to rivers, locally and globally. The final deliverable is a call-to-action digital story that is ostensibly being presented to either (1) the town council, if the river selected is local, or (2) a government environmental agency (in the United States, it would be the Environmental Protection Agency, or EPA), if the river is nonlocal. One requirement of this challenge is to interview an expert on river systems.

This challenge is designed to give students the tools to assess the basics of stream and river health so that as they continue to learn about climate change and anthropogenic threats to rivers, they have a solid understanding of the metrics that demonstrate disturbance and a basic understanding of the ripple effects of that disturbance ecologically and socioecologically.

Deliverables include:

- a call-to-action digital story
- an outline of research (at the teacher's discretion)
- a first-draft script (at the teacher's discretion)

Note: This challenge uses the term *river* throughout this project. The term is meant to include streams, tributaries, and any other form or size of flowing water; they are all important to understand, preserve, and protect.

## Assumptions and Logistics

**Time Frame:** This digital storytelling project takes place inside of a three- to four-week time frame.

**Length:** All digital stories should be under four minutes in length, unless otherwise specified.

**Slate:** All digital storytelling projects begin and end with the following slates:

- the title of the piece;
- the name of the authors, although it is strongly recommended that students do *not* put their last names on the piece either at the start or finish, during the credits;
- the wording *Permission Granted*, which gives your local school the right to publicly display the submission for educational purposes only, if desired; and
- all citations, references, and credits.

**Digital Rules/Literacy:** All students should follow the rules of digital citizenry in their proper usage and/or citation of images, music, and text taken from other sources. The Meridian Stories site has a comprehensive overview of applicable Digital Rules in the Meridian Resource Center.

## Process

Following is a suggested breakdown for the students' work. It is written addressed to the student teams so that you can use this language directly with them.

## Phase One

- Research and identify the key components that scientists use to measure the health of a river. Working with your teacher, create a list of metrics via which you can measure a river's health.

  (Teacher's option: Or you can share the following list and have students define what exactly is meant by each metric.) Metrics include, but are not limited to, the following:

  - → steady seasonal flows
  - → pollution sources, if any
  - → diverse biotic community
  - → nutrient cycling
  - → presence of native species and noninvasive species, if any
  - → stable riparian zones
  - → uninterrupted sediment transport
  - → nonsaline waters

- Choose a river about which to create your digital story (or this may be assigned). I recommend using a local river, if there is one, which will facilitate field work on that river. However, if there is not a river nearby, I recommend focusing on a regional river in order to ensure the full relevance of and connection to your work. (There is no problem with student teams working on the same river, perhaps measuring its health from different points.)
- Choose three metrics that will help establish the state of the river's health and determine how you will research the river inside of those three metrics. Here are three approaches, one of which is required.

  - → interviews with experts whose job it may be to monitor the river's health (this is required) or who are involved in some way with environmental health and sustainability
  - → internet- and library-based research

- ○ Keep in mind that we live in the age of big data, an age where data is being generated as never before, revealing new secrets about the nature of ecosystems and humanity's impact on the environment. Is there new data out there—data that may be about new standards or measuring techniques—that can assist you in determining the health of your river?

→ fieldwork, which may involve collecting river samples, making behavioral observations during different weather conditions, or both

- Using primary and secondary sources, research the health of your river inside of the three metrics you have selected.

  → Given that you are creating a *visual* call-to-action video, you may want to shoot your work during various parts of this research phase so that you have this footage available for your digital story. This is especially true for your interviews: be sure to get permission to shoot, record, and post your discussions with the interviewees.

- Create organizing charts and systems as necessary to keep track of your data, research, and conclusions.
- Prepare for the interviews. A call to action needs to have both data *and* people supporting it: people who live and breathe "river" or environmental ecosystems. This is why the interview is so important. The experts validate your research and call to action. And they help humanize your message, help provide an emotional connection to the topic for your audience. Identify your key interviewee.

  → Identify potential subject matter experts to be included. Keep in mind that this expertise often resides right there in your school in the science department.

  → Prioritize your list of potential subject matter experts to be interviewed and contact your interviewee. Once they have agreed to participate, be sure to prep them fully for the interview, to ensure their comfort and ease. This includes setting up a clear time and place ahead of time—you will want to scout locations—as well preparing them for the topic.

  → Additionally, in order to record and edit, your interviewee may need to sign a release form giving you permission to record, edit, and post this discussion online. Research generic and simple release forms online to find the right language for you.

- → Prepare your questions.

- Create an outline of the facts you have discovered inside of these three metrics that will form the spine of your call-to-action digital story, including a list of questions for your upcoming interview, which will be partially designed to fill out content areas where you don't have all the answers.

    - → Teacher's Option—Outline of Research: The teacher may require teams to hand in an outline of the information that they have discovered in these three areas as well as their interview questions.

- Conduct your interview and record it. Use a transcription app to move the words from the video recording to paper.
- Now, take your research that one last step and devise a plan of action. With the data you have, what can be done to improve the health of the river? Or perhaps the issue is this: what threats exist that could derail the current health of your river? So, this call to action could be more about, say, protecting the watershed that surrounds the river. Try to identify two or three clear action steps.
- Keep in mind that once you determine your action step, you may need to go back to your subject matter expert—the person you interviewed (perhaps there is more than one)—for one more round of interviews to learn more information about what is actionable and what isn't.

## Phase Two

- What *is* a call-to-action digital story? It is a short video that is designed to lead viewers on a quick journey from possible indifference to caring. Or from caring to actual action. That's a lot to ask of a short media piece. But this all suggests that this call to action digital story stays laser focused and builds its arguments well.
- Here is one way to consider structuring your story. As you look at each narrative section, brainstorm what the audience is *seeing* during that part of your digital story.

    - → Clearly identify the vast importance of the river to the local (or global) health of the region. This could span from economic health to recreational health, from food resource health to environmental health. Establish the critical importance of the river to the lives of your audience.

- → Introduce your issue. One way to do this is to present the question first: "Is our river healthy?" Or perhaps the question can be more specific: "Something is wrong with our river and we moved quickly to find out what." Here, you want to set up your story and invite the audience into wondering, "What did they discover?" This moment is your story hook.
- → Present your data. This may focus on what is healthy about your river . . . and what is not or what is threatening it . . . or what might happen if you don't act quickly. In terms of storytelling, this is your conflict.
- → Present your solution. This is the climax to the story: the moment that communicates to your audience, "This conflict can be solved; this threat can be averted; the fish can come back!"
    - That last line—"the fish can come back"—suggests the importance of bringing in the element of a live character. Whether it's a human character or an animal, your call to action will most likely have more impact if your audience can directly relate to an outcome that has a certain emotional appeal.
- → Present the call to action. This is the invitation to your audience to become a part of this success story. Or to become a part of the new behavior change needed to make this a success story. Or to become part of the defenses to avert the danger.

- Draft a script.
    - → Teacher's Option—First-Draft Script: The teacher may require teams to hand in their first-draft scripts for review and feedback.
- Storyboard the script. Creating a storyboard may be the most organized way to approach the logistics of shooting. This will help you organize the use of the footage that you have already taken, which will, in turn, identify what remaining shots you need. The primary purpose of creating a storyboard is to allow you to *see* your story—moment by moment—before shooting. When you see it in advance like that, you can make changes then, rather than after you have shot the whole thing (and discovered it doesn't make sense!).
- Preproduce the remainder of your story. This means gathering all the remaining materials you need to visualize your story. This might include scouting locations along the river or elsewhere; gathering props;

researching and collecting photos and footage; and checking on your video and sound recording devices.

- Rehearse your script. Finalize your script.
- Produce your story.

## Phase Three

- Record the voice-over or narration, as necessary.
- Edit the video, adding stills and graphics as desired.
- Postproduce the video, adding music and sound effects as desired.

## Media Support Resources

Figure 5–10

### Media Support: The Digital Storytelling Resource Center

Meridian Stories provides two forms of support for the student teams:

1. Meridian Innovators and Artists: This is a series of three- to four-minute videos featuring artists and innovative professionals who offer important advice in the areas of creativity and production.
2. Media Resource Collection: These are short documents that offer student teams key tips in the areas of creativity, production, game design, and digital citizenry.

I recommended that for this challenge, student teams review the following resources.

| Meridian Innovators and Artists | Media Resource Collection |
|---|---|
| Margaret Heffernan on Nonfiction | Producing: Time Management |
| Sarah Childress on Documentary Films | Creating Storyboards/Framing a Shot |
| Tom Pierce on Interviewing Techniques | Creating a Commercial/PSA |
| Tom Pierce on Editing | Conducting an Interview |

## Evaluation

Figure 5–11

### Rubric for Healthy Rivers: A Call to Action

| Content Command | |
|---|---|
| **Criteria** | **1–10** |
| The Metrics | The metrics upon which the digital story is focused are strong indicators of the river's health. |
| Research | The research and data presented reflect a thorough and substantive scientific investigation. |
| Call to Action | The proposed solution and call to action perfectly match the problem and the reality of what can be achieved. |

| Storytelling Command | |
|---|---|
| **Criteria** | **1–10** |
| Story Hook | The probing question that your video sought to answer—the hook—is set up in a convincing and inviting way. |
| The Interviews | The interviews are thoughtful, relevant, and compelling. |
| Story Structure | The narrative buildup to the climactic call to action is tight and engaging. |

| Digital Command | |
|---|---|
| **Criteria** | **1–10** |
| Editing | The call-to-action digital story is edited cleanly and effectively, resulting in an engaging viewing experience. |
| Sound and Music | Sound effects and music enhance the audience's engagement with the work. |
| Visualization | The choice of how to present the story and the quality of the visual mode reflect a thoughtful professionalism. |

| Human Skills Command | |
|---|---|
| **Criteria** | **1–10** |
| Collaborative Thinking | The group demonstrated flexibility in making compromises and valued the contributions of each group member. |

| Human Skills Command | |
|---|---|
| **Criteria** | **1–10** |
| Creativity and Innovation | The group brainstormed many inventive ideas and was able to evaluate, refine, and implement them effectively. |
| Initiative and Self-Direction | The group set attainable goals, worked independently, and managed their time effectively, demonstrating a disciplined commitment to the project. |

## Essential Questions

1. What factors affect water quality, aquatic health (animals and plants), and overall river sustainability?
2. How does climate change affect the health of a river?
    a. What does the term *anthropogenic* mean and why is it important to know?
3. How does one conduct effective scientific research that can lead to positive change?
    a. What are metrics and why are they important in scientific research?
4. How does one craft a realistic and inspiring call to action?
5. How has immersion in the creation of original content and the production of digital media—exercising one's creativity, critical thinking, and digital literacy skills—deepened the overall educational experience?
6. How has working on a team—practicing one's collaborative skills—changed the learning experience?

## Student Proficiencies

- Students will be able to identify important factors in river health.
- Students will be familiar with factors that might change river health. Students will be able to identify anthropogenic versus natural effects on rivers.
- Students will understand the importance of pursuing multiple research pathways in order to understand a complex, scientific issue. Students will be familiar with metrics to assess stream or river health.
- Students will gain an understanding of what the community can realistically do to create a healthy river system and craft that understanding into a persuasive message.

- Students will utilize key human skills, with a focus on creativity, critical thinking, and digital literacy, in their process of translating STEAM content into a new narrative format.
- Students will have an increased awareness of the challenges and rewards of team collaboration. Collaboration—the ability to work with others—is considered one of the most important human skills to develop in students as they prepare for life after secondary school.

## Curricular Correlations

This challenge addresses a range of curricular objectives that have been articulated by the Common Core Language Arts, Science and Technical Literacy Standards. In Figure 5-12 please find the standards that are addressed, either wholly or in part.

Figure 5–12

### Common Core State Standards for Language Arts and Science and Technical Literacy

| Standards | Eighth Grade | Ninth and Tenth Grades | Eleventh and Twelfth Grades |
|---|---|---|---|
| **W2**<br>**Writing**<br>**Text Types and Purposes** | Write informative/explanatory texts to examine a topic and convey ideas, concepts, and information through the selection, organization, and analysis of relevant content. | Write informative/explanatory texts to examine and convey complex ideas, concepts, and information clearly and accurately through the effective selection, organization, and analysis of content. | Write informative/explanatory texts to examine and convey complex ideas, concepts, and information clearly and accurately through the effective selection, organization, and analysis of content. |
| **W3**<br>**Writing**<br>**Text Types and Purposes** | Write narratives to develop real or imagined experiences or events using effective technique, relevant descriptive details, and well-structured event sequences. | Write narratives to develop real or imagined experiences or events using effective technique, well-chosen details, and well-structured event sequences. | Write narratives to develop real or imagined experiences or events using effective technique, well-chosen details, and well-structured event sequences. |

| Standards | Eighth Grade | Ninth and Tenth Grades | Eleventh and Twelfth Grades |
| --- | --- | --- | --- |
| **W4**<br><br>**Writing**<br><br>**Production and Distribution of Writing** | Produce clear and coherent writing in which the development, organization, and style are appropriate to task, purpose, and audience. | Produce clear and coherent writing in which the development, organization, and style are appropriate to task, purpose, and audience. | Produce clear and coherent writing in which the development, organization, and style are appropriate to task, purpose, and audience. |
| **W5**<br><br>**Writing**<br><br>**Production and Distribution of Writing** | With some guidance and support from peers and adults, develop and strengthen writing as needed by planning, revising, editing, rewriting, or trying a new approach, focusing on how well purpose and audience have been addressed. | Develop and strengthen writing as needed by planning, revising, editing, rewriting, or trying a new approach, focusing on addressing what is most significant for a specific purpose and audience. | Develop and strengthen writing as needed by planning, revising, editing, rewriting, or trying a new approach, focusing on addressing what is most significant for a specific purpose and audience. |
| **W7**<br><br>**Writing**<br><br>**Research to Build and Present Knowledge** | Conduct short research projects to answer a question (including a self-generated question), drawing on several sources and generating additional related, focused questions that allow for multiple avenues of exploration. | Conduct short as well as more sustained research projects to answer a question (including a self-generated question) or solve a problem; narrow or broaden the inquiry when appropriate; synthesize multiple sources on the subject, demonstrating understanding of the subject under investigation. | Conduct short as well as more sustained research projects to answer a question (including a self-generated question) or solve a problem; narrow or broaden the inquiry when appropriate; synthesize multiple sources on the subject, demonstrating understanding of the subject under investigation. |

*(continues)*

(continued)





| Standards | Eighth Grade | Ninth and Tenth Grades | Eleventh and Twelfth Grades |
|---|---|---|---|
| **RI 1**<br><br>**Reading Informational Text**<br><br>**Key Ideas and Details** | Cite the textual evidence that most strongly supports an analysis of what the text says explicitly as well as inferences drawn from the text. | Cite strong and thorough textual evidence to support analysis of what the text says explicitly as well as inferences drawn from the text. | Cite strong and thorough textual evidence to support analysis of what the text says explicitly as well as inferences drawn from the text, including determining where the text leaves matters uncertain. |
| **RST7**<br><br>**Science and Technical Literacy**<br><br>**Integration of Knowledge and Ideas** | Integrate quantitative or technical information expressed in words in a text with a version of that information expressed visually (e.g., in a flowchart, diagram, model, graph, or table). | Translate quantitative or technical information expressed in words in a text into visual form (e.g., a table or chart) and translate information expressed visually or mathematically (e.g., in an equation) into words. | Integrate and evaluate multiple sources of information presented in diverse formats and media (e.g., quantitative data, video, multimedia) in order to address a question or solve a problem. |
| **RST8**<br><br>**Science and Technical Literacy**<br><br>**Integration of Knowledge and Ideas** | Distinguish among facts, reasoned judgment based on research findings, and speculation in a text. | Assess the extent to which the reasoning and evidence in a text support the author's claim or a recommendation for solving a scientific or technical problem. | Evaluate the hypotheses, data, analysis, and conclusions in a science or technical text, verifying the data when possible and corroborating or challenging conclusions with other sources of information. |

PROJECT

# Rivers and Humanity: An Essay in Photos and Words

## A language arts challenge designed for middle and high school students

Figure 5–13

| Table of Contents | Range of Activities |
|---|---|
| • The Challenge<br>• Assumptions and Logistics<br>• Process<br>• Media Support Resources<br>• Evaluation<br>• Essential Questions<br>• Student Proficiencies<br>• Curricular Correlations | • Exploration of the nature-writing genre<br>• Nature writing based on river observations and reflections<br>• Creation of photographic essay based on river<br>• Digital literacy skills: video preproduction, production, and postproduction<br>• Human skills: creativity, collaboration, critical thinking, and presentational skills |

## The Challenge

In 1849, Henry David Thoreau wrote the following:

> The Mississippi, the Ganges, and the Nile, those journeying atoms from the Rocky Mountains, the Himmaleh, and Mountains of the Moon, have a kind of personal importance in the annals of the world. . . . Rivers must have been the guides which conducted the footsteps of the first travelers. They are the constant lure, when they flow by our doors, to distant enterprise and adventure, and, by a natural impulse, the dwellers on their banks will at length accompany their currents to the lowlands of the globe, or explore at their invitation the interior of continents. They are the natural highways of all nations, not only levelling the ground and removing obstacles from the path of the traveller, quenching his thirst and bearing him on their bosoms, but conducting him through the most interesting scenery, the most populous portions of the globe, and where the animal and vegetable kingdoms attain their greatest perfection.
>
> I had often stood on the banks of the Concord, watching the lapse of the current, an emblem of all progress, following the same law with the system, with time, and all that is made; the weeds at the bottom gently bending down the stream, shaken by

> the watery wind, still planted where their seeds had sunk, but erelong to die and go down likewise; the shining pebbles, not yet anxious to better their condition, the chips and weeds, and occasional logs and stems of trees that floated past, fulfilling their fate, were objects of singular interest to me, and at last I resolved to launch myself on its bosom and float whither it would bear me. (Thoreau 2003)

In these two paragraphs, Thoreau covers the sweeping range of ways that rivers shape, inspire, and assist humanity. From the great rivers of the world to his moment on the banks of the Concord River outside of Boston, Thoreau touches upon many attributes that make rivers such an elemental force in nature and in civilization.

In this challenge, following in the tradition of nature writing, students present a ten- to twelve-frame photographic story about a river. The photographic story needs to recorded original narration—250 to 400 words—and a minimum of ten of the photos must be original. This suggests that the river they are writing about is a local river (and by the word *river,* I mean to include streams or creeks or tributaries—any flowing body of water).

If you don't have a local river and students want to write about a world river—the Hudson, the Missouri, the Amazon, the Yangtze, the Rhine—they can still be very creative with original imagery that evokes the essence of the river. In other words, the photos don't have to be of the river itself. And the writing becomes more about how one imagines the Nile, for example, as based on reading first-person accounts, looking at Google Maps, and using other creative sources.

Deliverables include

- a photographic essay
- a first-draft essay in words and photos (at the teacher's discretion)

## Assumptions and Logistics

**Time Frame:** This digital storytelling project takes place inside of a three- to four-week time frame.

**Length:** All digital stories should be under four minutes in length, unless otherwise specified.

**Slate:** All digital storytelling projects begin and end with the following slates:

- the title of the piece;
- the name of the authors, although it is strongly recommended that students do *not* put their last names on the piece either at the start or finish, during the credits;
- the wording *Permission Granted,* which gives your local school the right to publicly display the submission for educational purposes only, if desired; and
- all citations, references, and credits.

**Digital Rules/Literacy:** All students should follow the rules of digital citizenry in their proper usage and/or citation of images, music, and text taken from other sources. The Meridian Stories site has a comprehensive overview of applicable Digital Rules in the Meridian Resource Center.

## Process

Following is a suggested breakdown for the students' work. It is written addressed to the student teams so that you can use this language directly with them.

## Phase One

- Begin by reading some renowned nature writers, in order to familiarize yourself with the history and essence of nature writing. Thoreau is certainly a favorite, starting with *Walden* (1854), his masterpiece. But there are many others who have excelled in this field who bring a very different sensibility, command of language, and cadence to their work. Consider these selections:
  - → *A Sand County Almanac*, by Aldo Leopold, 1949
  - → *Silent Spring*, by Rachel Carson, 1962
  - → *The Control of Nature*, by John McPhee, 1989
  - → *Feral*, by George Monbiot, 2013

  These are just a few suggestions of writers that use the sublime essences of nature as their foundation to explore the planet and humanity. Even reading a chapter of any of these books will expand your understanding of the possibilities for expression in this genre of writing.

### On Nature Writing

Nature writing is a genre of writing that seeks to elevate your relationship with the nature around you—and, by doing so, deepen your understanding of self and of humanity. That is your objective: to make your reader or viewer more aware of an essence—and there are many levels of essence, from literal beauty to sheer force and power, from metaphorical strengths to the wonder of biological minutiae—in their surroundings. In this case, you'll be focusing on the river. To do this—to help your audience interpret nature with fresh eyes and ears—consider ways to get outside to experience your topic: to feel, hear, and smell it. Write about those feelings, in the moment, like Thoreau does. And examine humanity's intersection with our natural surroundings as part of this experience. Often, they are inextricably linked, so explore that relationship. For that is often what's at the core of good nature writing: an investigation of how the beauty of nature outside of us enlightens the turmoil, confusion, curiosity, and wonder that we have inside of us.

- There is no prescribed way to approach this piece. This isn't a challenge that asks you to find a river, study it, and then write about how it makes you feel. But I've included some suggestions here to get you started.
- The first thing you need to do is identify your river. In particular, this may be about a very specific spot on the river—one that is private or one that is heavily traversed by foot traffic, perhaps with a bridge spanning it. Both spots yield different experiences. Or this could be about the general impact and character the river has on shaping your community and, perhaps, you and your team.
    - → If you are working on a nonlocal river, I recommend picking a river that fascinates you—that will invite you into its mysteries and wonder so that you can conjure a story about what river essences you have internalized.
- Go to the river, hopefully numerous times at different times of day and in different weather conditions. And when you are there, look *and listen*. Rivers often have a voice for you to discover. The more time you spend with the river, the more it will reveal to you. In this way, it may be helpful to think of this body of water as a character that you are getting to know. Try to leave time behind you and experience your river as deeply and as best as you can.
    - → You may want to use the sounds of the river as an underscore to your final piece. If that is the case, during one of your visits, record the sounds around you.
- As your exploration begins to take shape, it may be helpful to decide with which medium you want to lead: photography or the words? For example, will the story

come to you through your exploration with taking photographs? Or is the connection to the river taking place mostly inside of your mind in the form of words? Either way, with each visit, be sure to do both: take photos and write words.

- What are you actually writing about? There is no prescribed format here. But it's fair to say you are investigating, in words, two things: the river itself, literally and figuratively, and your relationship to this force of nature. How does it make you feel? What thoughts arise as a result of your time spent on this river?

  → If you are working on a nonlocal river, this essay in words and photos is less about traditional nature writing and more about the mash-up of ideas between the reality of your chosen river, as understood through research, and your imaginative understanding of this river, as informed by the river's history and storied past.

- Keep in mind that not all nature writing is about the beauty, majesty, and wonder of nature. Many rivers and streams are heavily polluted and damaged. That can be your story. It's an important one to tell.
- A second point to keep in mind: This challenge—this genre of expression—is as much about the authors and photographers as it is about the subject. The idea here is not to document the river; it's not to educate your audience about the river. No. It's about telling a story about your relationship to the river so that we, the audience, may also experience something new and energizing—so that we, in seeing the river through your eyes, have a new understanding. Why? Because you have done the work to get to know the river in ways that we, the audience, have not.
- By the end of the first phase, you should have several rounds of photos taken and several written passages or audio recordings (perhaps you recorded yourself) of your time at the river.

  → There is no harm in continuing to read nature-writing passages during this exploratory process to inspire you and open your eyes to what you are seeing. And I encourage you to use excerpts from other authors' works in your own essay (with the proper citation, of course).

- Much of this language assumes you are working as an individual and not as a team. If you are working as a team, all of the above applies. In this first phase, I recommend that each team member anchors their relationship and understanding of the river as an individual. It's in the next phase that the more collective experience begins.

## Phase Two

- Edit your words and pictures. Depending on your preference, you can begin with the pictures and move to the words. Or start with your words—your verbal story—and try to enhance those words with pictures. I recommend beginning with the photos. This is because a photographic story is often one that is told to you; it emerges from your editing process and is not pre-planned. Matching pictures to a written narrative often puts the photos in a secondary position. The goal in this challenge is for the words and photos to have equal power. As an experiment, try starting with the photos and see what story comes out of your editing process; you may discover a story that surprises you.
- Focus on the pictures. Create the first rough edit of your pictures. Maybe your team has fifty or perhaps over one hundred. Start to order them and see what story begins to evolve. Edit some out. Play around with order. Perhaps two stories evolve. Choose one or mix them into one. Have fun—this is like putting a puzzle together at the same time as designing it. The driving idea is to have each member of the team have an equal number of photos in the piece. Three thoughts to consider:
    - → Be sure to set up your photo editing process in a way that allows you to move the photos around into an order that begins to elicit a narrative.
    - → Some of the most compelling stories often come from photos that are not the best stand-alone works of art. Consider how the photos are in dialogue with each other: how one photo may lead to the next or refer back to an earlier photo through a repeating prop, similar lighting, or contrasting elements. In other words, your ten best photos may not be the ones for this essay.
    - → As your story evolves in this phase, make a list of the images that you think you want but don't have. You may want to shoot again.
- Focus on the words. Look at your various written pieces. Does a single narrative emerge? How are these different written entries from time spent on the river in dialogue with each other? Is there a story that you are trying to tell that is a shared experience among the team members? Or are there multiple stories—conflicting ones, perhaps—that need to find a way to cohere? Begin editing your written narrative, keeping in mind the pictures that you have selected, if that is the process you have already completed.

- → At this point it's worth asking this question if you haven't already: Where are you (your team) in this story?

- Create your first-draft essay in words and photos. Give it a tentative title; titling often gives stories a new shape. As you are doing this, begin to notice the different ways in which each medium communicates. Ask yourself, with each moment in your essay: Are the words getting closer to the truth of this moment or the pictures? As you answer that question, moment by moment, the story takes shape.

  - → Teacher's Option—First-Draft Essay in Words and Photos: Teachers may require that teams hand in their first draft for review and feedback.

- Reshoot and rewrite. Go back to your river one more time and with a story angle firmly in mind, take more pictures and write more thoughts. Perhaps just one more sentence. These may be pictures that you have identified that you need or pictures that result from further observation and exploration of this place. Keep in mind that not all pictures necessarily have to be of your subject.
- Edit again. Break down your story to between ten and twelve photos and order them. This is the point where you can look very carefully at each shot and ask yourself: Is it capturing all that I want it to capture? Does it need cropping or color correcting to maximize its impact? Similarly, edit your written story to between 250 and 400 words.

## Phase Three

- Focus on presentation. In the first step, rehearse reading your nature-writing piece along with presenting the pictures. The words and photos should be in dialogue with each other: the photos should make the words sparkle and the words should make us see the photos freshly—through your unique lens.
- This rehearsal process should kick out a few decisions that need to be made about presentation:
  - → Pacing: Do you want to present all the photos in an evenly timed fashion, accompanied by a steady voice reading from your written nature essay? Or should there be a slow buildup?
  - → Voicing: Who, actually, is giving voice to these words? And is it just one person or many? Might the team all speak together at some moment in the piece?

→ Music: Will you add music or a natural soundtrack to this essay presentation? Or does ambient silence serve this project best?

- Think about your digital tech options. There are many presentational programs that will allow you to press Start and let your show go forward in a pretimed fashion. You may want to use one of these programs or consider video recording a live presentation that cuts back and forth between your photos and you, or your team, reading your essay. In short, you can produce this as little or as much as you want.
- Based on all of the work so far, organize, record, and postproduce your piece: "Rivers and Humanity: An Essay in Words and Photos."

## Media Support Resources

**Figure 5–14**

### Media Support: The Digital Storytelling Resource Center

Meridian Stories provides two forms of support for the student teams:

1. Meridian Innovators and Artists: This is a series of three- to four-minute videos featuring artists and innovative professionals who offer important advice in the areas of creativity and production.
2. Media Resource Collection: These are short documents that offer student teams key tips in the areas of creativity, production, game design, and digital citizenry.

I recommend that for this challenge, student teams review the following resources.

| Meridian Innovators and Artists | Media Resource Collection |
|---|---|
| Margaret Heffernan on Nonfiction | Creating a Short Documentary |
| Liza Bakewell on Memoir and Nonfiction Writing | Sound Recording Basics |
| Michael Kolster on Photography | Sound Editing Basics |
| Chris Watkinson on Sound Design | Video Editing Basics |

## Evaluation

Figure 5–15

### Rubric for Rivers and Humanity: An Essay in Words and Photos

| Content Command | |
|---|---|
| **Criteria** | **1–10** |
| Nature-Writing Genre | The digital essay captures the essence of nature writing, giving the viewer a visceral understanding of the river and the essay's authors. |
| The River Through Words | The written script is an exemplar of nature writing, bringing new life and understanding to the landscape, the river. |
| The River Through Photos | The photographs are thoughtful and well constructed, and they effectively communicate important features of the river. |
| **Storytelling Command** | |
| **Criteria** | **1–10** |
| Word Choices | The specific choice of words—so critical in this disciplined genre of writing—are well chosen and evocative. |
| Photographic Story: Order | The photos, as presented in your order, communicate a compelling and thought-provoking narrative. |
| The Team or the Individual | The presence of the author-photographer-artists as the shapers of this experience is deeply felt. |
| **Digital Command** | |
| **Criteria** | **1–10** |
| Visual Presentation | Your choices in how you mixed the words and photos into a seamless visual narrative are creative and compelling. |
| Sound and Music | The choices around sound (or lack thereof) and music enhance the audience's engagement with the narrative. |

*(continues)*

(continued)



| Human Skills Command | |
|---|---|
| **Criteria** | **1–10** |
| Collaborative Thinking | The group demonstrated flexibility in making compromises and valued the contributions of each group member. |
| Creativity and Innovation | The group brainstormed many inventive ideas and was able to evaluate, refine, and implement them effectively. |
| Initiative and Self-Direction | The group set attainable goals, worked independently, and managed their time effectively, demonstrating a disciplined commitment to the project. |

## Essential Questions

1. What is nature writing?
2. Why is nature writing an important communicative form to experience?
3. Why are rivers so important to our literary and societal landscape?
4. How do photographs fundamentally differ from words as a mode of communication?
5. How can storytelling be used to more deeply understand complex educational ideas?
6. How has immersion in the creation of original content and the production of digital media—exercising one's creativity, critical thinking, and digital literacy skills—deepened the overall educational experience?

## Student Proficiencies

- The student will understand the essence of this genre of nonfiction writing.
- The student will empirically understand why this genre is important, for the individual and society.
- The student will gain a deeper understanding of the river as a literal and metaphorical entity of power and resonance.
- The student will understand and appreciate the deeply different ways that photos and words communicate ideas and story.

- The student will learn to utilize storytelling to communicate complex educational ideas in an engaging and immersive way.
- The student will utilize key human skills, with a focus on creativity, critical thinking, and digital literacy, in their process of translating one's relationship to a specific feature of nature into a new narrative format.

## Curricular Correlations

This challenge addresses a range of curricular objectives that have been articulated by the Common Core State Standards for English Language Arts. In Figure 5–16 please find the standards that are addressed, either wholly or in part.

Figure 5–16

**Common Core State Standards for English Language Arts**

| Standard | Eighth Grade | Ninth and Tenth Grades | Eleventh and Twelfth Grades |
|---|---|---|---|
| RL4<br><br>Reading and Literature<br><br>Craft and Structure | Determine the meaning of words and phrases as they are used in a text, including figurative and connotative meanings; analyze the impact of specific word choices on meaning and tone, including analogies or allusions to other texts. | Determine the meaning of words and phrases as they are used in the text, including figurative and connotative meanings; analyze the cumulative impact of specific word choices on meaning and tone (e.g., how the language evokes a sense of time and place; how it sets a formal or informal tone). | Determine the meaning of words and phrases as they are used in the text, including figurative and connotative meanings; analyze the impact of specific word choices on meaning and tone, including words with multiple meanings or language that is particularly fresh, engaging, or beautiful. (Include Shakespeare as well as other authors.) |

*(continues)*

*(continued)*

| Standard | Eighth Grade | Ninth and Tenth Grades | Eleventh and Twelfth Grades |
|---|---|---|---|
| W3<br>Writing<br>Text Types and Purposes | Write narratives to develop real or imagined experiences or events using effective technique, relevant descriptive details, and well-structured event sequences. | Write narratives to develop real or imagined experiences or events using effective technique, well-chosen details, and well-structured event sequences. | Write narratives to develop real or imagined experiences or events using effective technique, well-chosen details, and well-structured event sequences. |
| W4<br>Writing<br>Production and Distribution of Writing | Produce clear and coherent writing in which the development, organization, and style are appropriate to task, purpose, and audience. | Produce clear and coherent writing in which the development, organization, and style are appropriate to task, purpose, and audience. | Produce clear and coherent writing in which the development, organization, and style are appropriate to task, purpose, and audience. |
| W9<br>Writing<br>Research to Build and Present Knowledge | Draw evidence from literary or informational texts to support analysis, reflection, and research. | Draw evidence from literary or informational texts to support analysis, reflection, and research. | Draw evidence from literary or informational texts to support analysis, reflection, and research. |
| SL5<br>Speaking and Listening<br>Presentation of Knowledge and Ideas | Integrate multimedia and visual displays into presentations to clarify information, strengthen claims and evidence, and add interest. | Make strategic use of digital media (e.g., textual, graphical, audio, visual, and interactive elements) in presentations to enhance understanding of findings, reasoning, and evidence and to add interest. | Make strategic use of digital media (e.g., textual, graphical, audio, visual, and interactive elements) in presentations to enhance understanding of findings, reasoning, and evidence and to add interest. |

| Standard | Eighth Grade | Ninth and Tenth Grades | Eleventh and Twelfth Grades |
|---|---|---|---|
| SL6<br><br>Speaking and Listening<br><br>Presentation of Knowledge and Ideas | Adapt speech to a variety of contexts and tasks, demonstrating command of formal English when indicated or appropriate. | Adapt speech to a variety of contexts and tasks, demonstrating command of formal English when indicated or appropriate. | Adapt speech to a variety of contexts and tasks, demonstrating command of formal English when indicated or appropriate. |
| L3<br><br>Language<br><br>Knowledge of Language | Use knowledge of language and its conventions when writing, speaking, reading, or listening. | Apply knowledge of language to understand how language functions in different contexts, to make effective choices for meaning or style, and to comprehend more fully when reading or listening. | Apply knowledge of language to understand how language functions in different contexts, to make effective choices for meaning or style, and to comprehend more fully when reading or listening. |
| L5<br><br>Language<br><br>Vocabulary Acquisition and Use | Demonstrate understanding of figurative language, word relationships, and nuances in word meanings. | Demonstrate understanding of figurative language, word relationships, and nuances in word meanings. | Demonstrate understanding of figurative language, word relationships, and nuances in word meanings. |

PROJECT

# Rivers and Society: An Expo Fair

## A history challenge designed for middle and high school students

Figure 5–17

| Table of Contents | Range of Activities |
|---|---|
| • The Challenge<br>• Assumptions and Logistics<br>• Process<br>• Media Support Resources<br>• Evaluation<br>• Essential Questions<br>• Student Proficiencies<br>• Curricular Correlations | • Research on the intersection of societal development and rivers<br>• Research on selected historical innovations related to rivers<br>• Creation of a persuasive story about historical innovation<br>• Digital literacy skills: video preproduction, production, and postproduction<br>• Human skills: creativity, collaboration, critical thinking, and presentational skills |

## The Challenge

This challenge looks at rivers from a historical and economic perspective, trying to get at this essential question: Why have humans historically flocked to rivers? Rivers have provided a steady source of food and water for humanity for as long as there have been humans. But over time, humanity turned more and more to the power of rivers to innovate and progress. What critical inventions revolutionized their time by finding new ways to put the river to use? How has the power of rivers guided humanity and, equally important, how have we changed the rivers to meet our own needs?

In order to explore these questions, students will focus on a particular human-made innovation or river utilization—for example, the waterwheel, canal, logging, canoe—that had the effect of making the river facilitate humanity's survival and well-being.

Student teams pick one product or usage. They are at the Regional Annual River Expo, where people are hawking all sorts of river-related products . . . in the time period of their choice. They have the stage for three or four minutes. They must create a pitch video about their product. Tell them they're free to dress up and present from the time period in which the innovation or utilization was taking place.

Deliverables include

- a digital story
- an outline of research (at the teacher's discretion)
- a first-draft script (at the teacher's discretion)

## Assumptions and Logistics

**Time Frame:** This digital storytelling project takes place inside of a three- to four-week time frame.

**Length:** All digital stories should be under four minutes in length, unless otherwise specified.

**Slate:** All digital storytelling projects begin and end with the following slates:

- the title of the piece;
- the name of the authors, although it is strongly recommended that students do *not* put their last names on the piece either at the start or finish, during the credits;
- the wording *Permission Granted*, which gives your local school the right to publicly display the submission for educational purposes only, if desired; and
- all citations, references and credits.

**Digital Rules/Literacy:** All students should follow the rules of digital citizenry in their proper usage and/or citation of images, music, and text taken from other sources. The Meridian Stories site has a comprehensive overview of applicable Digital Rules in the Meridian Resource Center.

### Process

Following is a suggested breakdown for the students' work. It is written addressed to the student teams so that you can use this language directly with them.

### Phase One

- Research an overview of rivers and their historical intersection with humanity. If you are studying a particular geographic location or time period in class, limit your research to within those parameters. Identify a specific function that interests you for how a river was used to help society survive or progress. Here's a list of ideas to get you started:
    - → waterwheel
    - → different types of paddle craft

- sailing ships
- nets or fishing poles
- dams
- hydroelectric power
- aqueducts
- logging
- turbines

- Using primary and secondary sources, research three different facets of your innovation.
  - What It Is: If it's a thing, like a waterwheel, what actually is it and how does it work?
  - Its Origin: When and where was it discovered or first put to use? What was the need that led to its invention? What problem did the river and its elements solve?
    - Keep in mind that your select innovation doesn't have to be one that changed the world. It could be a local use on a local river that changed the historical development of your region.
  - Successful Examples: Find some effective examples of the application of your selected innovation. This will help you to determine the economic impact of your innovation; the flaws (where it failed in its first trial runs); and what innovations were made to make the innovation more efficient and effective.

    The story you are going to tell—your pitch at the local tech expo—does not have to take place right at the very moment your innovation was invented. For example, dams might have been around for ten years before this expo. They just haven't been around where you live. They might be new to your area. What is important is that you have enough information about the early beginnings of your innovation to be able to sell it based on proof of its efficacy in terms of improving the human condition.

- Create an outline of the facts you have uncovered in these three areas.
  - Teacher's Option—Outline of Research: The teacher may require teams to hand in an outline of the information that they have discovered in these three areas.

One more thing to note: You most likely know a lot more about this innovation than the character you are about to create, who will be selling this use of the river. Why? Because you live now and have access to a lot more information. For example, you know how much power a dam can actually create, but you also know the damage it can do to the river's ecosystem. Feel free to include this information—what you now know—in your pitch video in some creative way.

## Phase Two

- Brainstorm about the general shape of your video. Some directions to consider:
  - Story Shape: This is about selling a product or a way of life. You could design the whole video like a commercial. That is an option. Or you could record one person doing a sales pitch, as if to an audience of people standing around, waiting to sign on the dotted line and purchase. And keep in mind: What's one of the best-selling strategies? A good story.
  - Story Arc: This challenge is *not* about creating a period video. You can set it in any time. It *is* about being accurate about the river use on which you are focusing and letting the audience know (1) what it is; (2) what problem it solves; (3) how it works; and (4) the positive outcome it produces. If there are also negative outcomes—such as the damage dams do to a river's natural ecosystem mentioned earlier—then find a way to hint at that information to let the viewer know that *you* know! (This could be featured, for example, in an exchange with a skeptical buyer who is listening to your pitch.)
  - Location: It's an expo. Like a trade show. Perhaps you set it in contemporary times. Or in the time period of your subject. Either way, here are some decisions to make about location:
    - Are you working out of a booth?
    - Will you be on a stage for a three-minute presentation?
    - Or are you just showing a video (which I am giving you permission to do, even though video may not have been invented in that time period) that is designed like a commercial?
  - Character and Voice: Who, if anyone, is doing the selling? Is this being voiced like an old-fashioned auctioneer or in the cool tones of a

contemporary person who sounds and looks like they should be selling you an expensive watch but in fact is introducing you to a new kind of boat called a . . . kayak?

- Create an outline of your story, fusing the key points you identified in your research outline with the general creative approach that you have just brainstormed.
- Create a first-draft script. Two things to consider:
  - → This script is designed to sell and persuade as well as communicate truthfully the assets and benefits of this innovation.
  - → The core driver to this is the river as a powerful and beautiful product of nature. Don't ignore the qualities and potency and lure of this elemental force.
    - ○ Teacher's Option—First-Draft Script: The teacher may require teams to hand in a first-draft script for review and feedback.
- Preproduce your story. This means gathering all the materials you need to visualize your story. This might include scouting locations; gathering props; researching and collecting photos and footage; making costumes; casting characters; and checking on your video and sound recording devices.
  - → If you are shooting scenes in one or more locations, creating a storyboard may be the most organized way to approach the logistics of shooting.
- Rehearse your script. Finalize your script.
- Produce your story.

## Phase Three

- Record the voice-over or narration, as necessary.
- Edit the video, adding stills and graphics as desired.
- Postproduce the video, adding music and sound effects as desired, keeping in mind the effect that music—in terms of enhancing the emotions, triumphs, and suspenseful tone of the story—can have on the audience.

## Media Support Resources

Figure 5–18

### Media Support:
### The Digital Storytelling Resource Center

Meridian Stories provides two forms of support for the student teams:

1. Meridian Innovators and Artists: This is a series of three- to four-minute videos featuring artists and innovative professionals who offer important advice in the areas of creativity and production.
2. Media Resource Collection: These are short documents that offer student teams key tips in the areas of creativity, production, game design, and digital citizenry.

I recommend that for this challenge, student teams review the following resources.

| Meridian Innovators and Artists | Media Resource Collection |
| --- | --- |
| Margaret Heffernan on Nonfiction | Creative Brainstorming Techniques |
| Liza Bakewell on Memoir and Nonfiction Writing | Creating a Commercial/PSA |
| Janet McTeer on Acting for Film and Stage | Creating Storyboards/Framing a Shot |
| Tom Pierce on Editing | Video Editing Basics |

## Evaluation

Figure 5–19

### Rubric for Rivers and Society: An Expo Fair

| Content Command | |
|---|---|
| **Criteria** | **1–10** |
| The River Innovation | The choice of innovation is rich, complex, thoughtful, and thoroughly explained. |
| The Origins Story | The presentation of how this innovation came to be is well researched. |
| The Usefulness and Impact | The usefulness of this innovation—its potential to contribute to human progress—is clearly and accurately stated. |
| **Storytelling Command** | |
| **Criteria** | **1–10** |
| The Pitch | The narrative is persuasive: the organization of the facts makes for a compelling argument. |
| The Story Arc | The narrative is engaging: the elements of story are clear and pull the audience into the experience. |
| The Characters and Voice | The verbal presentation of your pitch—the voice and characters—is inviting and alluring. |
| **Digital Command** | |
| **Criteria** | **1–10** |
| Visualization | The choice of how to present the story and the quality of the visuals reflect a thoughtful professionalism. |
| Editing | The digital story is edited cleanly and effectively, resulting in an engaging viewing experience. |
| Sound and Music | Sound effects and music enhance the audience's engagement with the scene and its persuasive qualities. |

| Human Skills Command | |
|---|---|
| **Criteria** | **1–10** |
| Collaborative Thinking | The group demonstrated flexibility in making compromises and valued the contributions of each group member. |
| Creativity and Innovation | The group brainstormed many inventive ideas and was able to evaluate, refine, and implement them effectively. |
| Initiative and Self-Direction | The group set attainable goals, worked independently, and managed their time effectively, demonstrating a disciplined commitment to the project. |

## Essential Questions

1. What role have rivers played in humanity's historical quest for survival and progress?
2. How has information gathered from primary sources enhanced your understanding of the topic? How is the information from the primary sources different from the information gathered from secondary sources?
3. What is one innovation that utilized the river and all its natural elements that impacted the evolution of societal development locally, regionally, or globally?
4. How does one construct a persuasive story about an innovative idea that leads viewers to accept and value that innovative idea?
5. How has immersion in the creation of original content and the production of digital media—exercising one's creativity, critical thinking, and digital literacy skills—deepened the overall educational experience?
6. How has working on a team—practicing one's collaborative skills—changed the learning experience?

## Student Proficiencies

- The student will begin to conceptualize the deeply intertwined histories of humanity and river systems, with a focus on intersections around mechanical power, transportation, commerce, and food.
- The student will understand how combining primary and secondary sources can help one to reach a more complex and nuanced understanding of history.

- The student will learn about one specific river innovation within the context of the historical time in which it came to be impactful.
- The student will have organized a persuasive narrative about the assets and potency of this selected river innovation.
- The student will utilize key human skills, with a focus on creativity, critical thinking, and digital literacy, in their process of translating historical content into a new narrative format.
- The student will have an increased awareness of the challenges and rewards of team collaboration. Collaboration—the ability to work with others—is considered one of the most important human skills to develop in students as they prepare for life after secondary school.

## Curricular Correlations

This challenge addresses a range of curricular objectives that have been articulated by the Common Core State Standards for English Language Arts and History/Social Studies and by the C3 Framework from the National Council of Social Studies. In Figures 5–20 and 5–21, please find the standards that are addressed, either wholly or in part.

Figure 5–20

**Common Core State Standards for English Language Arts Standards and History/Social Studies**

| The Standard | Eighth Grade | Ninth and Tenth Grades | Eleventh and Twelfth Grades |
|---|---|---|---|
| RI1<br><br>Reading Informational Text<br><br>Key Ideas and Details | Cite the textual evidence that most strongly supports an analysis of what the text says explicitly as well as inferences drawn from the text. | Cite strong and thorough textual evidence to support analysis of what the text says explicitly as well as inferences drawn from the text. | Cite strong and thorough textual evidence to support analysis of what the text says explicitly as well as inferences drawn from the text, including determining where the text leaves matters uncertain. |

| The Standard | Eighth Grade | Ninth and Tenth Grades | Eleventh and Twelfth Grades |
|---|---|---|---|
| W2<br>Writing<br>Text Types and Purposes | Write informative/explanatory texts to examine a topic and convey ideas, concepts, and information through the selection, organization, and analysis of relevant content. | Write informative/explanatory texts to examine and convey complex ideas, concepts, and information clearly and accurately through the effective selection, organization, and analysis of content. | Write informative/explanatory texts to examine and convey complex ideas, concepts, and information clearly and accurately through the effective selection, organization, and analysis of content. |
| W3<br>Writing<br>Text Types and Purposes | Write narratives to develop real or imagined experiences or events using effective technique, relevant descriptive details, and well-structured event sequences. | Write narratives to develop real or imagined experiences or events using effective technique, well-chosen details, and well-structured event sequences. | Write narratives to develop real or imagined experiences or events using effective technique, well-chosen details, and well-structured event sequences. |
| W4<br>Writing<br>Production and Distribution of Writing | Produce clear and coherent writing in which the development, organization, and style are appropriate to task, purpose, and audience. | Produce clear and coherent writing in which the development, organization, and style are appropriate to task, purpose, and audience. | Produce clear and coherent writing in which the development, organization, and style are appropriate to task, purpose, and audience. |
| W5<br>Writing<br>Production and Distribution of Writing | With some guidance and support from peers and adults, develop and strengthen writing as needed by planning, revising, editing, rewriting, or trying a new approach, focusing on how well purpose and audience have been addressed. | Develop and strengthen writing as needed by planning, revising, editing, rewriting, or trying a new approach, focusing on addressing what is most significant for a specific purpose and audience. | Develop and strengthen writing as needed by planning, revising, editing, rewriting, or trying a new approach, focusing on addressing what is most significant for a specific purpose and audience. |

*(continues)*

*(continued)*

| The Standard | Eighth Grade | Ninth and Tenth Grades | Eleventh and Twelfth Grades |
|---|---|---|---|
| **W7**<br>**Writing**<br>**Research to Build and Present Knowledge** | Conduct short research projects to answer a question (including a self-generated question), drawing on several sources and generating additional related, focused questions that allow for multiple avenues of exploration. | Conduct short as well as more sustained research projects to answer a question (including a self-generated question) or solve a problem; narrow or broaden the inquiry when appropriate; synthesize multiple sources on the subject, demonstrating understanding of the subject under investigation. | Conduct short as well as more sustained research projects to answer a question (including a self-generated question) or solve a problem; narrow or broaden the inquiry when appropriate; synthesize multiple sources on the subject, demonstrating understanding of the subject under investigation. |
| **SL1**<br>**Speaking and Listening**<br>**Comprehension and Collaboration** | Engage effectively in a range of collaborative discussions (one-on-one, in groups, and teacher-led) with diverse partners on grade 8 topics, texts, and issues, building on others' ideas and expressing their own clearly. | Initiate and participate effectively in a range of collaborative discussions (one-on-one, in groups, and teacher-led) with diverse partners on grades 9–10 topics, texts, and issues, building on others' ideas and expressing their own clearly and persuasively. | Initiate and participate effectively in a range of collaborative discussions (one-on-one, in groups, and teacher-led) with diverse partners on grades 11–12 topics, texts, and issues, building on others' ideas and expressing their own clearly and persuasively. |
| **SL5**<br>**Speaking and Listening**<br>**Presentation of Knowledge and Ideas** | Integrate multimedia and visual displays into presentations to clarify information, strengthen claims and evidence, and add interest. | Make strategic use of digital media (e.g., textual, graphical, audio, visual, and interactive elements) in presentations to enhance understanding of findings, reasoning, and evidence and to add interest. | Make strategic use of digital media (e.g., textual, graphical, audio, visual, and interactive elements) in presentations to enhance understanding of findings, reasoning, and evidence and to add interest. |

| The Standard | Eighth Grade | Ninth and Tenth Grades | Eleventh and Twelfth Grades |
|---|---|---|---|
| SL6<br><br>Speaking and Listening<br><br>Presentation of Knowledge and Ideas | Adapt speech to a variety of contexts and tasks, demonstrating command of formal English when indicated or appropriate. | Adapt speech to a variety of contexts and tasks, demonstrating command of formal English when indicated or appropriate. | Adapt speech to a variety of contexts and tasks, demonstrating command of formal English when indicated or appropriate. |
| L3<br><br>Language<br><br>Knowledge of Language | Use knowledge of language and its conventions when writing, speaking, reading, or listening. | Apply knowledge of language to understand how language functions in different contexts, to make effective choices for meaning or style, and to comprehend more fully when reading or listening. | Apply knowledge of language to understand how language functions in different contexts, to make effective choices for meaning or style, and to comprehend more fully when reading or listening. |
| RH2<br><br>History/Social Studies<br><br>Key Ideas and Details | Determine the central ideas or information of a primary or secondary source; provide an accurate summary of the source distinct from prior knowledge or opinions. | Determine the central ideas or information of a primary or secondary source; provide an accurate summary of how key events or ideas develop over the course of the text. | Determine the central ideas or information of a primary or secondary source; provide an accurate summary that makes clear the relationships among the key details and ideas. |
| RH9<br><br>History/Social Studies<br><br>Integration of Knowledge and Ideas | Analyze the relationship between a primary and secondary source on the same topic. | Compare and contrast treatments of the same topic in several primary and secondary sources. | Integrate information from diverse sources, both primary and secondary, into a coherent understanding of an idea or event, noting discrepancies among sources. |

Figure 5–21

## C3 Framework by the National Council of Social Studies

| Sixth Through Eighth Grade | Ninth Through Twelfth Grade |
|---|---|
| *D1.5.6-8.* Determine the kinds of sources that will be helpful in answering compelling and supporting questions, taking into consideration multiple points of views represented in the sources. | *D1.5.9-12.* Determine the kinds of sources that will be helpful in answering compelling and supporting questions, taking into consideration multiple points of view represented in the sources, the types of sources available, and the potential uses of the sources. |
| *D2.Civ.14.6-8.* Compare historical and contemporary means of changing societies and promoting the common good. | *D2.Civ.14.9-12.* Analyze historical, contemporary, and emerging means of changing societies, promoting the common good, and protecting rights. |
| *D2.Geo.4.6-8.* Explain how cultural patterns and economic decisions influence environments and the daily lives of people in both nearby and distant places. | *D2.Geo.4.9-12.* Analyze relationships and interactions within and between human and physical systems to explain reciprocal influences that occur among them. |
| *D2.Geo.6.6-8.* Explain how the physical and human characteristics of places and regions are connected to human identities and cultures. | *D2.Geo.6.9-12.* Evaluate the impact of human settlement activities on the environmental and cultural characteristics of specific places and regions. |
| *D2.Geo.7.6-8.* Explain how changes in transportation and communication technology influence the spatial connections among human settlements and affect the diffusion of ideas and cultural practices. | *D2.Geo.7.9-12.* Analyze the reciprocal nature of how historical events and the spatial diffusion of ideas, technologies, and cultural practices have influenced migration patterns and the distribution of human population. |
| *D2.Geo.8.6-8.* Analyze how relationships between humans and environments extend or contract spatial patterns of settlement and movement. | *D2.Geo.8.9-12.* Evaluate the impact of economic activities and political decisions on spatial patterns within and among urban, suburban, and rural regions. |

| Sixth Through Eighth Grade | Ninth Through Twelfth Grade |
|---|---|
| *D2.Geo.11.6-8.* Explain how the relationship between the environmental characteristics of places and production of goods influences the spatial patterns of world trade. | *D2.Geo.11.9-12.* Evaluate how economic globalization and the expanding use of scarce resources contribute to conflict and cooperation within and among countries. |
| *D2.His.2.6-8.* Classify series of historical events and developments as examples of change and/or continuity. | *D2.His.2.9-12.* Analyze change and continuity in historical eras. |

National Council for the Social Studies (NCSS), The College, Career, and Civic Life (C3) Framework for Social Studies State Standards: Guidance for Enhancing the Rigor of K–12 Civics, Economics, Geography, and History (Silver Spring, MD: NCSS, 2013).

Please note that a link to student digital storytelling work that supports and complements the ideas and activities in this chapter can be found at www.meridianstories.com.

# References

American Psychological Association (APA). 2002. *Developing Adolescents: A Reference for Professionals*. Washington, DC: APA. https://www.apa.org/pi/families/resources/develop.pdf.

Anderson, Monica, and Jingjing Jiang. 2018. *Teens, Social Media and Technology 2018*. Washington, DC: Pew Research Center. https://www.pewresearch.org/internet/wp-content/uploads/sites/9/2018/05/PI_2018.05.31_TeensTech_FINAL.pdf.

Beckford, Avil. 2018. "The Skills You Need to Succeed in 2020." *Forbes* (website), August 6. https://www.forbes.com/sites/ellevate/2018/08/06/the-skills-you-need-to-succeed-in-2020/.

Blau, Andrew. 2005. *Deep Focus: A Report on the Future of Independent Media*. San Francisco: National Alliance for Media Arts and Culture. https://issuu.com/namac/docs/namac_deep_focus.

Brenner, Grant Hilary. 2019. "Do People Use YouTubers to Replace Real Relationships?" *ExperiMentations* (blog), May 20. https://www.psychologytoday.com/blog/experimentations/201905/do-people-use-youtubers-replace-real-relationships.

Brown University. n.d. "Admission and Aid." Brown University (website). Accessed November 29, 2021. https://www.brown.edu/admission.

Buford, Bill. 1996. "The Seductions of Story Telling." *The New Yorker*, June 24: 11. https://www.newyorker.com/magazine/1996/06/24/the-seductions-of-story-telling.

Cakebread, Caroline. 2017. "People Will Take 1.2 Trillion Digital Photos This Year—Thanks to Smartphones." Business Insider, August 31. https://www.businessinsider.com/12-trillion-photos-to-be-taken-in-2017-thanks-to-smartphones-chart-2017-8.

Carson, Rachel. 2002. *Silent Spring*. Boston, MA. Mariner Books.

Creasy, Rob. 2018. "Seeing Education as a Process." In *The Taming of Education: Evaluating Contemporary Approaches to Learning and Teaching*, edited by Rob Creasy, 1–9. Cham, Switzerland: Springer International. https://doi.org/10.1007/978-3-319-62247-7_1.

Dweck, Carol. 2014. "The Power of Believing That You Can Improve." Filmed September 2014 in Norrköping, Sweden. TED video, 10:24. https://www.youtube.com/watch?v=_X0mgOOSpLU.

———. 2013. *Zero to Eight: Children's Media Use in America in 2013*. San Francisco: Common Sense Media. https://d2e111jq13me73.cloudfront.net/sites/default/files/research/zero-to-eight-2013.pdf.

———. 2017. *The Common Sense Census: Media Use by Kids Age Zero to Eight, 2017*. San Francisco: Common Sense Media. https://www.commonsensemedia.org/sites/default/files/uploads/research/csm_zerotoeight_fullreport_release_2.pdf.

Rideout, Victoria, and Robert Mann. 2019. *The Common Sense Census: Media Use by Tweens and Teens, 2019*. San Francisco: Common Sense Media. https://www.commonsensemedia.org/sites/default/files/uploads/research/2019-census-8-to-18-full-report-updated.pdf.

Rideout, Victoria, and Michael Robb. 2020. *The Common Sense Census: Media Use by Kids Age Zero to Eight, 2020*. San Francisco: Common Sense Media. https://www.commonsensemedia.org/sites/default/files/uploads/research/2020_zero_to_eight_census_final_web.pdf.

Ritchhart, Ron, and David Perkins. 2008. "Making Thinking Visible." *Educational Leadership* 65 (5): 57–61.

Robinson, Andrew. 2007. *The Story of Writing: Alphabets, Hieroglyphs and Pictograms*. London: Thames and Hudson.

Ross, David. 2020. "Reflections on Project-Based Learning." Interview by Tom Farmer. eSchool News, November 2. https://www.eschoolnews.com/2020/11/02/reflections-on-project-based-learning/.

Search for Common Ground. 1999. "Introduction to the Curriculum." *Nashe Maalo.*

Share Your Learning. n.d. "Presentation of Learning." Share Your Learning. Accessed June 15, 2021. https://shareyourlearning.org/pol/.

Sontag, Susan. 1977. *On Photography*. New York: Macmillan.

Talbert, Robert. 2018. "What Does the Research Say About Flipped Learning." Robert Talbert, Ph.D. (website), March 1. http://rtalbert.org/what-does-the-research-say/.

Teaching and Learning Lab. n.d. "Design Thinking in Education." Harvard University (website). Accessed October 20, 2020. https://tll.gse.harvard.edu/design-thinking.

This American Life. n.d. "Overview." This American Life (website). Accessed June 28, 2021. https://www.thisamericanlife.org/about.

Thoreau, Henry David. 2003. *A Week on the Concord and Merrimack Rivers*. Project Gutenberg ebook 4232. Project Gutenberg (website). Last updated December 22, 2019. https://www.gutenberg.org/files/4232/4232-h/4232-h.htm.

TikTok. 2020. "Creator Communities." *TikTok Creator Portal* (blog), December 28. https://www.tiktok.com/creators/creator-portal/en-us/tiktok-content-strategy/creator-communities/.

Trei, Lisa. 2007. "New Study Yields Instructive Results on How Mindset Affects Learning." Stanford News, February 7. http://news.stanford.edu/news/2007/february7/dweck-020707.html.

Twain, Mark. 2006. "How to Tell a Story and Others." Project Gutenberg ebook 3250. Project Gutenberg (website). Last updated May 25, 2018. https://www.gutenberg.org/files/3250/3250-h/3250-h.htm.

Umoh, Ruth. 2017. "Want to Score a Job at Microsoft, Facebook, IBM or Amazon? Here Are Top Tips from Their HR Execs." CNBC Make It, November 29. https://www.cnbc.com/2017/11/29/heres-how-to-score-a-job-at-microsoft-facebook-ibm-and-amazon.html.

United States Institute of Peace. 2010. "Proposed General Objectives for the Iraqi Youth Media Project."

Vygotsky, L. S. 2004. "Imagination and Creativity in Childhood." *Journal of Russian and East European Psychology* 42 (1): 7–97.

Wikipedia. 2020. "6–3–5 Brainwriting." Wikipedia, March 30. https://en.wikipedia.org/wiki/6-3-5_Brainwriting.

Wilson, Edward. 2017. *The Origins of Creativity*. New York: Liveright Publishing.

WNYC Studios. n.d. "Come Through with Rebecca Carroll." WNYC Studios (website). Accessed November 29, 2021. https://www.wnycstudios.org/shows/come-through/about.

YouTube. n.d. "YouTube for Press." *YouTube Official Blog*. Accessed November 19, 2021. https://blog.youtube/press/.

Zhou, Dave. 2017. "What I Look For . . ." IDEO.org, March. https://www.ideo.org/perspective/what-i-look-for-1.